Awakening Journey
of the
Bride

by

Rochelle Butler

Awakening Journey of the Bride

Copyright © 2024 by Rochelle Butler

ISBN: 979-8989686353 (sc)
ISBN: 979-8989686360 (e)

Riverview Press

info@riverview-press.com
www.riverview-press.com

DEDICATION

This Book is dedicated to the ladies of Warrior Alley Bible Study.

> Tiffany Butler
>
> Kristina Gott
>
> Darla Doward
>
> Carmen Coates

It is and has been my pleasure and I thank you all for allowing the God in me to be presented to you by way of teaching and instruction in the word and life expression.

I pray that Christ may be formed in you continually.

I'd also like to dedicate this book to those in my family at New Covenant Ministries. You have been a constant oasis for me both physically and spiritually. May you forever be blessed of the Lord and know how dear and special you are to me.

I would be remiss if I did not thank Sharlene Claytor who has been a wonderful prayer covering over my life. Thanks immensely.

Lastly I would like to thank my cousin Mildred Lee who has been a great friend and support. She has such a giving heart to bless others. May she be blessed to the degree she has blessed me and others. May she know how special she is and how greatly loved.

PREFACE

The Awakening Journey of the Bride! *is a book of passion as one running after her lover. The Shulamite woman in the book of Song of Solomon, realizing she has a wedding day coming, sets about to prepare. She was constantly on a search for her lover, the bridegroom, the one she loves. Most likely, when she started out she did not know what the cost of love would be and that changes would have to be made before a marriage took place. This more or less is a picture of my life. Though I was raised in a church, I heard very little if any about the topic of the church as being the bride of Christ or that preparation would have to be made to meet Christ, the bridegroom. Moreover, I never heard that the bride is the one who makes herself ready, with the help of the Holy Spirit. I heard my grandmother, who was a Pentecostal woman of God, always proclaiming 'Jesus is coming soon,' but I can't ever remember her saying, "The bride must make herself ready" as opposed to "'Be ready." Oh yes, there is a difference.*

Over the years of walking with the Lord on a wilderness journey, he began to unveil to me the necessary journey of preparation. He said in his word that he is coming back for a church without spot, wrinkle, blemish or any such thing. This gives a clear indication that preparation is necessary to remove the spots, wrinkles and blemishes. The church, as well as Christ, both play a part in the preparation process, and yes, it is a process. My passion over the years is to come to *know* Christ, not just know *about* Christ. My desire is to know not only the gifts but the giver of the gifts. Not merely to know the things of God but rather, the God of all things. It's a daily journey unto preparation. As Christ arises in us, so does his light of understanding and awakening arise. As the word says, "Line on line, precept on precept." Little by little, the Lord leads us on this journey of preparations and becoming one with him in union and covenant.

We can see all through the Bible how much it speaks of marriage. In Ephesians 5:25, Paul tells us, "Husbands, love your wives, just as Christ loved the church and gave himself up for her." Christ's love for the church is in representation of marriage both physically and spiritually. Jesus' first miracle was performed at a marriage. In the book of Genesis, we see the communion Adam and Eve had with one another and with Christ. In the last book of the Bible, Revelation, Christ is speaking through John to the seven churches of Ephesus, Smyrna, Pergamos, Thyatira, Sardis, Philadelphia and lastly Laodicea. There were seven letters to the seven churches. Each church had specific instructions and corrections that needed to be made if they were to be with him. The church of Philadelphia was the only one that was in right standing. We are the church and representation of a bride. We all will choose what type of bride we will be based on our relationship with Christ and by allowing his dealings and corrections within our hearts. I have been and will continue to be on that type of journey until I leave this earth. There have been good days and bad days on this journey because submission and change are not always easy. My grandfather Belcher used to always say "May not be good *to* you, but it's good *for* you." I thank God for the loving enduring father he is and I'm thankful he has been with me on this journey of becoming. Christ will forever be at work in our lives, taking us from glory to glory, molding us to be compatible with him in his glory and the glory that he is, and his glory yet to be revealed.

Christ's intent, and my intent in writing this book under his direction, is to make it simple for the reader to understand, just as Christ spoke and taught his disciples in parables. Parables are short stories of life with great impact and meaning. The *Awakening Journey* up and get dressed for her groom, and finally, clear the path for the groom to return.

Today is the day of readiness, salvation and preparation. As we see the darkness setting in, it's time for us to allow the Christ within to arise. Look up church, for our redemption draws nigh! Hallelujah! Let's get this journey started! May you too become dressed in readiness and hasten his coming. Maranatha, come Lord Jesus.

of the Bride is a sequel to my first book *Awaken Oh Bride* and, like the first book, is also to be used as a toolbox. Though you or I may not need every tool in the box, we will at some point need a tool. The topics written here-in deal with a Bridal Journey unto preparation and relationship with Christ. I have tried to set forth examples of those that have gone before us with regards to what to do and what not to do. It is my hope that we will fine-tune our lives and give clarity on how to make ourselves ready. This book has been written to be practical and compatible with our everyday living. The majority of topics, but not all, will include specifics on all things related to what is necessary for a spiritual wedding as it relates to a natural wedding. I'm certain some of the information may be new to some and not so new to others, however, it has been God-inspired for the topics included. I have found that time is one of the biggest thieves in our lives, and if not careful, we will just assume we always have tomorrow. Nothing can be further from the truth.

For that reason, I have written in journal form. The journals written are only a small portion of the vast wisdom and knowledge of God in reference to bridal preparation. I mean, to be honest, who is qualified to express in writing about Christ the awesome wonder that he is? I have found the only way it can be expressed is through experiencing Christ in relationship. Only then does he become real and made alive off the pages of any book written, primarily the written word of God. These journals are just a start and a small peek into the light of Christ. Proverbs 25:2 tells us "It is the Glory of God to conceal a matter; but the honor of kings is to search out a matter." Your part will be to search the scriptures prayerfully and find out how Christ deals with you as he prepares and makes you ready. All of us will have a wedding gown and will need to be dressed appropriately, first inwardly to outwardly, as the kingdom of God is within and not to be observed, as the scriptures declared.

To sum it all up: My mandate from the Lord and Sound the Trumpet Ministries is to sound the trumpet, alert the bride to wake

TABLE OF CONTENTS

INTRODUCTION

This generation is likened unto the apologue describing what happens if you put a frog in a pot of boiling water. It will immediately leap out. But if the pot is full of tepid water and is gradually heated up, the frog will remain in the water until it boils to death. This truth is in comparison to a parable. A parable is a short and simple story that teaches religious precepts for life. Parables convey spiritual truths with everyday examples of life and are great tools for life and living. I am sure you have heard the saying "It was so simple I almost missed it," or "Hiding in plain sight." If not careful, the simple truth of parables can be missed.

Throughout the Gospels, Jesus taught his disciples in parables so they could comprehend his message. Yet those who were not his missed it because it was hidden. The Bible gives us clear instruction on how we should be conducting our lives in these latter times. The Lord spoke of what manner of man we ought to be as we see the day of his return approaching. The message in this book, *Awakening Journey of the Bride!*, is directed toward the church and those who realize we are living in perilous times. We are in a time of great darkness that has never been seen before in our generation. We cannot be as the frog in the boiling pot of hot water. The water is heating up and I'm afraid if we're not careful we will miss our awakening moment and lose our chance to jump out of the boiling pot.

If we are awakened, we can see that the water temperature is continually rising and almost to a boiling point in our society. I'm sure some are wondering, "What exactly are you talking about?" As we look around in our nation, we can see the America we love and once knew is gradually slipping away. Our children are being targeted, our right to choose is slowly being taken away, our freedom of speech is being silenced and we have accepted it without much resistance. The frog of society has become comfortable in the warming water. It doesn't realize it is slowly dying.

The present church mirrors that of the Laodicean church John spoke of in Revelation. It has become self-centered and comfortable in its earthly achievements. There has been very little transformation in the lives of people whereby Christ can be seen and made manifest in our congregations and nation. Matthew 5:13 says, "Ye are the salt of the earth; but if the salt has lost his savor, wherewith shall it be salted? It is thenceforth good for nothing but to be cast out, and to be trodden under foot of men." So, my question is, if the church is the salt and light of the earth, why are the nations of the earth, our cities and communities so dark? Somewhere we, the church, the people of God, have lost our savor.

It's time we awaken and arise in this moment of time. It's time we agree with Paul the Apostle who cried, "I travail that Christ might be formed in you." Paul's concern was about a people that graduated from mere children of God to Sons and Daughters. A people in full stature and representation of Christ. If I may ask, how often have you heard the cross being preached in its significance in the life of the believer? The cross will bring a total extinction and annihilation of one's self. I usually hear it most at resurrection or Easter Sunday. The cross is all about total surrender and submission to Christ, where our lives are no longer our own and we live only for what God wills, not what we want, desire, or think we deserve. The cross is a daily way of life. News flash Saints! It is time for the church to return to God and his eternal will and plan. It is time the church be not as the frog and slowly die in the pot of comfortability because it doesn't like confronting evil. There's no other way.

God is in the process of preparing a people and drawing them back unto himself. His desire is that he may fill us up with himself and become the light to invade the current darkness. Nothing of this earth that is built can do that. Sorry if these truths offend. It's time for the church to wake up and accept the truth if we are expecting to go with God in these end times.

Awaken means to arouse one's self. Awakening has to do with disruption that sometimes challenges us in our comfortability, challenges us in our comfort zone. We are just going along, not creating havoc for the kingdom of darkness the way the kingdom of darkness has created havoc for our lives, our families and the nation. The word says Jesus came to destroy the works of the devil and we ought not to be comfortable with him destroying without a fight.

It's interesting; in reality people who sleep walk have no idea they are doing so. They need to be awakened or aroused. Christ is wakening and arousing his church. Let us arise.

The darkness has overtaken the light that should be shining bright in the church. When I speak of the church, I am not firstly speaking of the building but we the people who *are* the church, the house of God. I have penned this book in hope that a people will awaken and understand preparation is necessary for the church to become the bride Christ intended it to be. It is a daily preparation and the journey will require a daily pursuit of God, asking him to draw and apprehend us. Daily moments of awakening are necessary. Awakening may not happen all at once but moment by moment, day by day, the light of Christ will dawn on our hearts. We must allow him to help us understand his parables of life. This book is in no way meant to be critical but to awaken. Therefore the trumpet must be sounded as an alert.

I look forward to you taking this daily journey with me. This book was also written in hope that it will cause you to consider what you are thinking about, what preoccupies your life in reference to what matters most. Are you running for an earthly crown or an eternal crown?

Christ is who should matter most from the standpoint of the scriptures. This book is a sequel of my book *Awaken Oh Bride*. Let's get this journey started and move on in our journey with Christ. Let's allow him to cause moments of awakening in our lives unto change and transformation. Please don't be the frog that stayed in the pot. The journey with Christ begins today. For some, let's pick up where we left off. How about that? It's time to get moving or keep it moving. We have a wedding coming. Our Bridegroom is standing at the door. Be blessed now and always. Enjoy the journey. Christ awaits you!

 *Let the Journey Begin!*

*"Don't be afraid to take that
First step, because it could be
The beginning of many
Great things."*
Roger Lee

The Trumpet

O ften in this book you will see a phrase and the question, 'Can you hear the sounding of the trumpet?' The symbolism of the trumpet in the Bible when sounded represented many things, such as an alert, warning or announcement.

In ancient Israel they used a Shofar. The Shofar has a unique sound, an awakening arising sound. A sound that commands attention. A good example can be found in Ezekiel 33:3-5.

³If when he seeth the sword come upon the land, he blows the trumpet, and warn the people;

⁴Then whosoever heareth the sound of the trumpet, and taketh not warning; if the sword come, and take him away, his blood shall be upon his own head.

⁵He heard the sound of the trumpet, and took not warning; his blood shall be upon him. But he that taketh warning shall deliver his soul.

Some years back, the Lord directed me as to how he would use me in these end-times. He said, "Your ministry will be one of awakening, to awaken people in reference to the days and times we are living." Preparation is daily and necessary to be ready to meet him. The Lord then posed a question to me. "If you see a child in the middle of the road and cars are coming at him, would you whisper, 'Get out of the street.'? Or would you shout 'GET OUT OF THE STREET'?" He then said, "My children are in the street and cars are coming." Simply put, most, if not all, are unaware of the times. There is more to being a Christian than merely saying "I am a Christian." Many have stopped at salvation, but that's only the beginning. When we accept Christ there is a change from the inside out. We used to sing a song years ago – "Jesus on the inside, working on the outside. Oh what a change in my life."

Along my journey the Lord has given me many illustrations to help me understand his word and what he is relating to me. One in particular is the comparison of the caterpillar and the butterfly. Salvation is like a caterpillar, the beginning. It is our acceptance of Christ and our ongoing relationship with Christ that leads us to becoming a butterfly. It is through a journey unto transformation. It is the removal of the former life unto a new life in Christ. There is journey between the two. A deep personal intimate relationship with Christ is meant to transform us into his likeness. It's to let the Christ within be unleashed in and through us. That is beyond our power to do, but as we yield and submit our lives to him, he brings it all to pass. II Corinthians 5:7 *"If any man be in Christ, he is a new creature. Old things are passed away, behold all things become new."*

While there is yet time, I encourage each of us to take inventory of our lives. Christ is alerting his church. Now is the time of preparation. As we take inventory of our lives, we ask ourselves, "Are we the same person we were when we first accepted Christ?" Christ in us is Christ through us. God is looking for the life of his son in all of us.

Saul, on the road to Damascus in Acts chapter 9 once encountered God and was no longer the same. Before meeting Christ, he was a murderer of Christian. After he met Christ, Saul the murderer became Paul the Apostle. We read nothing of his former life. He journeyed with the Lord unto a deep personal committed relationship and wrote many of his epistles while in prison. He was no longer the caterpillar but changed into the butterfly. That's the way our lives should be as we journey.

In closing, this book is symbolism of a trumpet. Christ is sounding an awakening, a warning. Look up! Our redemption draws nigh. John the Baptist came out of the wilderness preaching and proclaiming "Repent ye, for the kingdom of heaven is at hand." His trumpet sounded. Repent. There is one coming.

I understand this book may not be for everyone. However, I am reminded of a mother who is able to recognize the voice of her child. Even out of thousands of voices, if her son or daughter calls for her, she knows the sound of her child's voice. So it is with this book. The voice of the Lord is calling and all who are his children will recognize the voice of their father calling. Let he who has ears, hear what the Spirit of the Lord is saying to the church.

The trumpet is sounding. Can you hear it?

 *The Invitation*

I think it is so befitting from the onset to start the book with the invitation. I am inviting you to go along with me on this journey of preparation too meet our Bridegroom. I'm inviting you but only the Holy Spirit, our helper, is the one that can prepare us. I can't think of a better time as we look out over the horizon of our nation and the nations of the earth. More closely, we can peer into our communities and states and see the fast and vast shift of change. We are in a day and time when it is detrimental for us not to stop and take notice. The handwriting on the wall was for Belshazzar in the book of Daniel. The king decided to host a party, during which he drank out of the golden vessels that were dedicated to God. Suddenly, a hand was seen writing on the wall. A hand, with no body attached! In Daniel chapter five we read, *"The king's countenance was changed, and his thoughts troubled him, so that the joints of his loins were loosed, and his knees smote one against another."* Belshazzar had a shock and awe moment that made it impossible for him not to stop and take notice of the signs and wonders before him. The king called upon Daniel, who had the gift of interpreting dreams, to come and tell him what the handwriting meant. It was a warning. "Thou art weighed in the balances, and art found wanting."

It is no different for us. The handwriting is on the wall for us, too. The signs of the times that are before us and times we are now living in are very troubling, to say the least. It is impossible for our thoughts not to be concerned or troubled and ask, "What meanest this, Lord?" The scripture clearly tells us in Luke 21:25-28:

25"And there shall be signs in the sun, and in the moon, and in the stars; and upon the earth distress of nations, with perplexity; the sea and the waves roaring;

26Men's hearts failing them for fear, and for looking after those things which are coming on the earth: for the powers of heaven shall be shaken.

27And then shall they see the Son of man coming in a cloud with power and great glory.

28And when these things begin to come to pass, then look up, and lift up your heads; for your redemption draweth nigh."

Hallelujah! Our redemption draws nigh! What a day of rejoicing that will be, but yet also a day of war. Why war? Because nothing is ever handed to us; we have to fight our way till the end. Fight! Yes, because we have an enemy who opposes God and us and he knows his end is near.

So, you may ask, what is this invitation all about? The meaning of invitation according to Webster is an often formal request to be present or participate. We are now living in the end times that the Bible spoke so clearly about. Christ is coming back for his Bride without spot, wrinkle or blemish. How about that? But before I get into the shouting, I understand there is a process of being made ready which will challenge us in the way we live and the decisions we make. As I said earlier, it will require us to fight. I find the first fight for me has been fighting for the Christ within to remain and not be uprooted by flesh, which is my mind, will and emotions. There is only one person that would love for that to happen, and I'm sure you guessed who it is. Our enemy is Satan. His goal is and has always been to sever the relationship between Christ and man. You may ask, "Why will I have to fight?" The Bible says in Ephesians 6 that we are not fighting against flesh and blood but principalities, powers and rulers of darkness. We will have to overcome to reign with Christ. How we live our lives daily and the decisions we make will dictate how victorious or defeated we will be. Focusing back on the invitation, the scripture reads:

Luke 14:16-24 ¹⁶Then said he unto him, A certain man made a great supper, and bade many:

¹⁷And sent his servant at supper time to say to them that were bidden, Come; for all things are now ready.

¹⁸And they all with one consent began to make excuse. The first said unto him, I have bought a piece of ground, and I must needs go and see it: I pray thee have me excused.

¹⁹And another said, I have bought five yoke of oxen, and I go to prove them: I pray thee have me excused.

²⁰And another said, I have married a wife, and therefore I cannot come.

²¹So that servant came, and shewed his lord these things. Then the master of the house being angry said to his servant, go out quickly into the streets and lanes of the city, and bring in hither the poor, and the maimed, and the halt, and the blind.

²²And the servant said, Lord, it is done as thou hast commanded, and yet there is room.

²³And the lord said unto the servant, go out into the highways and hedges, and compel them to come in, that my house may be filled.

²⁴For I say unto you, that none of those men which were bidden shall taste of my supper.

Brother Luke's gospel is an admonishment to us, jam-packed with much instruction for our times as it was for his. I am sure we can find ourselves in the passage, especially when it comes to excuses. Just as Christ sent his servant to them to come, he first invited his own and it's no different for us today. He is sounding a clarion call which means a strongly expressed demand or request for action. Our action is to come out to him, meet him anew, and dine with him in preparation for the big wedding day.

The scriptures revealed they all began to make excuses. Believe me, I get it! I've done it plenty of times along my journey with the Lord, though not always intentionally. Nonetheless, I have learned to pay attention to the times and season of God spiritually speaking in my own life, as well as corporately. God moves a certain way in certain times and seasons, as he did in John 5:4 when the angel went down to the pool of Bethesda to stir the water at a certain time. Whoever stepped in first was healed. Imagine if someone was not aware of that time. How they would have missed their opportunity to be healed! Living in the Spirit is so important because without the spirit, we can miss so much of what God has for us. Let us awaken.

I believe had the servants known spiritually what time it was, their choices and decisions would have been different. Perhaps what seemed so important at that time may not have been after all. The profound thing that stands out to me is that their excuses didn't seem like excuses to them, but rather something that needed to be done. I see from the consequences their excuses were not a priority to God. It's been said that man does not see as God sees. So true! Unfortunately, they missed their day of visitation and opportunity by not accepting the invitation. From a little child up, I have always heard the older saints say, 'God always has his own." How true! The Lord sent his servant to extend the invitation out to the hedges and highways and compel them to come, which is where God had his own. The first shall be last and the last shall be first. Right now, in this time, place and space, Christ is bidding us to come and dine with him in preparation that we might be made ready. And not only to be made ready but simply to fellowship with us. We are his creation and he loves us and wants to be so close to us. He is our heavenly father and cares much for us.

I'm reminded of the quote by Lao Tzu: "The journey of a thousand miles begins with one step." What a transforming statement! So it is with us in our journey walking with the Lord. The beautiful part, what

I really love about this statement, is that so much can be accomplished in that first step. One step is moving forward. It is one step of saying, "Yes Lord, I want to be made ready for our big day." That 'yes Lord' will cost us everything, the losing of our own lives for Christ's life. As Paul said, *"Nevertheless, not I but Christ in me."* (Galations 2:20) Christ does the work, but we have to fight because we have an enemy opposing us on every side. But in order for us to reign with him, we must be overcomers. We learn that along our journey we will face temptations, tests and trials. But we have read the end of the book and know we will win!. Because of the Christ within, the fight will be worth it.

My prayer for us today is that we come out to meet the bridegroom unto preparation and never will remain the same. May we not miss our day of visitation and invitation. The time is now! Let us pray.

Heavenly father, today we hear your clarion call and ask that you would draw us and we will come running. We want to reflect you in this world and be made ready. We want to be a bride made ready to meet you. Please give us hearts to hear clearly what you are saying to the churches. Open our eyes so we can see with your vision. Go deep within my heart, Lord. I give you permission to change me and make me new. I trust you in the journey and ask that you would make your presence known in me. Make me a useful vessel in your hand for these end times. May I seek you daily and never be the same. I give you my all. In Jesus name I pray.

Come on! Let's take the first step in this thousand mile journey unto eternity, no more to be the same!

Come Dine With Me

I'm sure you've seen those TV episodes where a person wins a chance to spend a day with a famous person such as a music entertainer, a sports personality or some big dignitary. I am sure one would spend countless hours thinking on the questions they plan to ask, especially ones you are most inquisitive about. However, once you are in their presence, you forget everything because of the awe and excitement of spending time with them. Somehow everything falls in place and all your questions are answered. I am a firm believer of body language. All that the inquiring mind wants to know is all out the window. The sheer joy of fellowship and spending time with someone you truly admire overrides everything you could have ever planned.

So what if Jesus, the most famous person in the world, said, *"I am coming to your house today,"* like he did to Zacchaeus in Luke 19:5? How exciting would that be? I'm sure most of us would be overwhelmed, honored, and totally exuberant that Jesus, the most famous person in the world, would come and see me, little old me! But guess what? We have that opportunity everyday though perhaps not literally in body. He lives in us; he is a real person and is concerned about us deeply and most intimately. As we see the day of his coming approaching and so much darkness on the horizon, he desires we become closer and closer to him. Hearing his voice is a must for specific direction in order to navigate in these perilous times.

Christ is knocking at the door of our hearts just as he knocked at the door of the Laodicean church. He wants to come dine with us. When I hear the word 'dine,' I am drawn to a most romantic setting with fine dining. The table is spread with fine linens, beautiful crystal and gleaming place settings. Delicious delicacies of all types of foods are presented for my enjoyment. It's common that while dining in romantic settings, unforgettable memories are made. Imagine a marriage proposal or the announcement of a promotion or maybe a pregnancy. In that setting, secrets are shared, there is a personal exchange of thoughts, and desires are revealed. Heart to heart affection is expressed between two lovers or close intimate friends. Lovers draw away for special and intimate occasions. Memories are made that will forever be imprinted on the hearts.

Christ is calling us to dine with him. He has secrets to share with us. He said he makes all things known unto his friends. He is a personal and intimate God who desires and requires our full attention. He loves us affectionately.

In the book of Luke 12:35-36 we read:

[35]Let your loins be girded about, and your lights burning;

[36]And ye yourselves like unto men that wait for their lord, when he will return from the wedding; that when he cometh and knocketh, they may open unto him immediately.

I believe Christ is drawing us even deeper unto him so that we may learn of him. Christ desires that we learn his ways and recognize his voice so when he knocks we will open immediately. We are waiting before him in our times of prayer and dining with him. Dining in love, unity and oneness are creating an abiding bond between us and Christ. We each give of ourselves.

Life has many distractions. Everyday life things, which are necessary, can distract us from our fellowship time with Christ. We must be watchful that the doing of things remains in its rightful place in our lives, a balance. Things that come out of balance become distractions. Life can become so full, without even trying. I am drawn back to the early days of my relationship with Christ and learning to walk with him. I had so many things going on that little by little those things began to crowd Christ out. My personal intimate time with him became less and less and I became less effective for him. I would be so tired by the time it was time for me to pray and study my Bible that sometimes it just didn't happen at all. My head was cluttered with everything but him and I could not hear his call to come and dine. I found out over time it was impossible for me to say "I love you Jesus." Even though I was doing things for him, because I was not spending time with him, I really didn't know him but only of him. We cannot afford to miss our daily time of dining with the Lord. Daily is the keyword. How can we love someone we truly don't know? In these perilous times, end time days, our lives must be balanced. The devil our enemy thrives on distracting us and wasting our time. Yes, he can waste our time doing good things, but are they God things? Meaning is this what Christ has led me to do?

Remember what Paul said in II Corinthians 10:23:

23 *You say, "I am allowed to do anything,"[a] but not everything is good for you. You say, "I am allowed to do anything," but not everything is beneficial.*

I believe the importance of a personal relationship with Christ can never be overstated. I teach this point often and always. I have been in different circles of believers who have never been taught or see the need of a personal relationship with Christ, even though they have a relationship with church, church activities and so much more. But I must reiterate that we *must* have an intimate personal relationship with Christ if we are his. It is impossible to love someone who you don't really know. You must recognize their voice, and that happens with familiarity. We must come and dine. It's a part of preparation unto the big day.

Let's be like the Shulamite woman in Song of Solomon 5:2:

²*"One night as I was sleeping, my heart awakened in a dream. I heard the voice of my beloved; he was knocking at my bedroom door. 'Open to me, my darling, my lover, my lovely dove,' he said, 'for I have been out in the night and am covered with dew.'"*

Christ knocked on the door of her heart because he wanted to fellowship and be with her. Oh, how he loves us in such a caring and intimate fashion. As the father told his son Jesus, *"I in you and you in me. May they become one as we are one."* (John 14:20) Dining and fellowshipping with the master are all about becoming one with him in will, thought and intent. We were created for him and him alone. Oh, how he loves us, his bride. It's high time we make him our priority. Hear the knock on the door of our hearts. Knock, knock, who's there? Jesus, the Son of the living God. Will you come and dine with him today?

They Shall Be Mine

Many times, when I am asleep, the Lord will commune with my spirit. Sometimes I dream and other times it is a phrase, a word, or a scripture that has left an indelible impression in my spirit.

For the most part, this happens when the battles of life have brought me to a place of being tired and weary. Though yet pursuing Christ in the midst of my fatigue, my spiritual armor has taken some hits. I felt as though I had come up short in some things. Christ is most gracious to me when he shows up this way and shuts down all my mental wonderings and when I am looking for answers.

As I retired for the night, the Lord spoke Malachi 3:17 in my spirit. *"And they shall be mine, saith the Lord of hosts, in that day when I make up my jewels, and I will spare them, as a man spareth his own son that serveth him."* As I began to study and ponder on the word of the Lord, my spirit was encouraged as well as enlightened. What a word! I mean, the Lord thinks I am a jewel? And he will spare me? A jewel is a precious stone. I am overwhelmed at the unfathomable love of God for his church, the bride, his people. God's care and concern for us is without measure.

I have often wondered, "Lord, I sure hope I am going to be ready for our big day." Maybe you have thought about that too. I mean, some days I take one step forward and seem to fall back five. But the

Lord reminds me man does not see as God does. Life is a big obstacle course for us to learn, grow and mature. Training for reigning is not always what we expect. What we think is apparent defeat is but a lesson to be learned and mastered.

As I continued to go forward in my study of the word the Lord had given, I went to Isaiah 62 and oh my! What a word! Isaiah says that you and I have been highly prized and purchased. We were worth dying for! He says, *"I will not rest until you his bride's righteousness and vindication goes forth."* Of course he is speaking of Christ's righteousness because we have no righteousness of our own. Christ says you shall be called by a new name which signifies covenant. For example, he made a covenant with Abraham, and changed his name, (Genesis 17:5). In Revelation 22:4 it tells us that God's name shall be on our foreheads, indicating that we belong to him. We are his and he is our bridegroom. One might ask what a name represents. A name speaks of character, fame, reputation and a new status. Those of us who belong to Christ, who have his name, will have the character and reputation that his name represents. Let's name a few of the characteristics of Jesus: pure, holy, just, righteous, loving, humble, tender hearted, meek, gentle, forgiving, undefiled, and so many more. You can add to the list. My, what a mighty God we serve!

The word of the Lord through Isaiah 62:3 says, *"You shall be a crown of glory and honor in the hand of the Lord, a royal diadem."* WOW! The definition of diadem is a jeweled crown or headband worn as a symbol of sovereignty. Plain and simple, it is the tiara of a king. What can be said? Oh, my word, this is what our God thinks of us, his bride. He has placed us in his hands which means we are secure in him, regardless of what we face along our daily journey of awakening.

Now! The question must be asked, do we ourselves feel the same way toward our God? Is he our prize possession and jewel? Is he the tiara about my head that signifies I am his and he is mine? Does my life speak of the representation of his life in nature and character? When someone sees me, can they tell that I am different because I belong to him and his tiara is shining brightly with his name on my forehead? Is he worth dying for daily? Is he worth me laying my life down that he may live? I know this is a heavy question which brings much reality and consideration. This question must be answered so, if necessary, changes can be made while it is yet day.

In closing, let's take another step in our journey and briefly glance at a final point of Isaiah 62:4-5. The Lord was letting Israel know that they would no longer be forsaken. Their time of restoration had come in spite of their falling away. He called them Hephzibah, which is the amplified version means 'my delight in her' and Beulah, which means 'married, owned and protected by the Lord.' Isn't that beautiful? It has always been about the father preparing a bride for himself and he is willing to go to any lengths to do it. The bridegroom rejoices over the bride and his banner over her is love.

This is a beautiful passage of scripture that depicts restoration and an opportunity that was given for a people to return to the father. Today we have that same opportunity. God is still restoring relationships. In referring back to my beginning scripture in Malachi 3:17, we read. *"When I make up my jewels and I will spare them, as a man spareth his own son that serveth him."* God will preserve them, pardon them and accept them. Also, God will separate and discriminate between those who are his and those who are not in the day he makes up his jewels. This gives clear indication that not everyone will be a jewel. The qualification is that we must be ALL and ONLY his, wholehearted in our love of relationship with him. That is the beauty of relationship and marriage. Who would want to marry someone who has other lovers? There would be no need for marriage. It's kind of what I would call 'shacking and packing.' What do I mean? I'm referring to people who live together without the commitment of marriage. Marriage is about commitment.

Perhaps you may have wandered off the path which leads to life in Christ. Perhaps you have drifted from your covenant of marriage with him and need to return back and delight once again in the father.

Perhaps your love has grown cold through the journey of life and you have but a flicker of light left. I encourage you today and remind you that you are the jewel and royal diadem Christ created. He is waiting and would love for you to allow him to finish the work he started in you. He knows how to remove the filthy rags of our righteousness and clothe us in *his* righteousness. Will you become his and only his today? Say yes!

Let's pray:

Thank you father, for loving us so much that you made us your crown jewels. Forgive us that we have not always shined for you and loved you the way you have loved us. I ask that you touch every cold indifferent place in our hearts today and rekindle our first love for you. Please help us to become willing vessels, that you may finish the work you started in us. May you, the consuming fire, set a fire in us that can't be contained or controlled; a fire that will drive out all forms of darkness and complacency in our lives from this day forward. Teach us how to love you and give us an increase of love for you. Thanks now and forevermore for being a good father who loves us immensely. In Jesus' name we pray. Amen!

Betrothal

In days of my youth, my friends and I would always talk about the 'big day' - our weddings! How exciting it would be for someone you care so deeply for to 'pop the question'. Those four little words, 'will you marry me' were like magic words for us! We would talk about all the different scenarios of how we would like the proposal to be presented. Maybe he would drop an engagement ring into my glass at a fine restaurant. Maybe he would hire a skywriter, put up a billboard, or provide a violin serenade to set the scene perfectly. We thought about how exciting that moment would be. In reality, we knew the proposal was only the beginning. It would be the first step. But the answer, 'Yes, I will marry you," is not the final 'I do take thee.' We knew there is journey between those two statements. A journey of knowing and growing to know one another, to love one another as well as to make sure each other is their perfect fit. I find that time really does prove all things.

When I think of betrothal, I am reminded of Mary and Joseph's relationship. Talk about 'time proves all things!' I mean, the Lord put both of them in a very trying situation that led them to trust him against all odds. I can only imagine all the whispers and gossip that was going around.

Let's take a look at Luke 1:27-35.

[27]To a virgin espoused to a man whose name was Joseph, of the house of David; and the virgin's name was Mary.

[28]And the angel came in unto her, and said, Hail, thou that art highly favoured, the Lord is with thee: blessed art thou among women.

[29]And when she saw him, she was troubled at his saying, and cast in her mind what manner of salutation this should be.

[30]And the angel said unto her, Fear not, Mary: for thou hast found favour with God.

[31]And, behold, thou shalt conceive in thy womb, and bring forth a son, and shalt call his name Jesus.

[32]He shall be great, and shall be called the Son of the Highest: and the Lord God shall give unto him the throne of his father David:

[33]And he shall reign over the house of Jacob for ever; and of his kingdom there shall be no end.

[34]Then said Mary unto the angel, How shall this be, seeing I know not a man?

[35]And the angel answered and said unto her, The Holy Ghost shall come upon thee, and the power of the Highest shall overshadow thee: therefore also that holy this which shall be born of thee shall be called The Son of God."

We see from this portion of scripture that Mary was not yet married to Joseph but only engaged or betrothed to him. The meaning of betrothal in the Ultimate Bible Dictionary is 'an act of engagement for marriage.' In Bible time, betrothal was as binding as marriage. In Biblical terms, 'betrothal' and 'espousal' were almost synonymous with marriage and as binding. WOW! I take this statement as marriage almost being as good as done when one is in betrothal.

Betrothal is the same as being engaged. In a relational aspect, I like to think of engagement as interaction and exchange between two lovers. An exchange of love, ideas, thoughts, feelings, likes, dislikes, plans, purposes and pursuits of the union they are about to embark upon for life. I believe in this period is where the two are on their way to becoming one and testing if they are really meant to be together. It's a time to learn what they both really want out of marriage and not merely the title of being married. I am reminded when I used to attend many weddings in the early 70's, after the ceremony was over and the two walked down the aisle as husband and wife, before they completely exited the church, there was a broom and they both jumped over to complete the matrimony. However, now looking in hindsight, I believe the betrothal period is where we should jump the broom. I believe commitment and covenant is made during that period and that final 'I do' is the outcome of that covenant. In betrothal, our love for one another is tried, proven and tested as we commit to one another through thick and thin that our love will be proven stronger that any outside forces that come against our love, be it family, friends, sickness or anything else. God's love endures all things.

I have come to the conclusion that TV is a weapon of mass deception with its episodes of such things as the Bachelor and Bachelorette. Programs such as these give the idea that you can find love in a matter of days by going on numerous dates, committing godless intimate acts, while at the same time competing with many other women. What a demonic presentation of marriage, not at all the way our God ordained it. Unfortunately, many in the world and yes, in the church, have fallen into traps like this. This is simply a trap of the enemy. Remember the frog in the boiling water? Too many are becoming complacent, unaware that the water is heating up.

Let's get back to betrothal, which is simply preparation for the big day. Just as a natural bride will search for the perfect gown, so it is with the Lord as he said in Ephesians 5:26-27. The bride prepares to adorn herself in a most beautiful, elegant fashion and looks to find the perfect shoes to match her beautiful gown. In Ephesians 6:15, Paul speaks of our feet being shod with the preparation of the gospel of peace. Christ will be and is the peace in every storm. On our betrothal journey, we will encounter storms. But Christ is our peace. Finally in the preparation process, the bride looks for the perfect crown, the tiara. I so love the tiara Christ has crowned us with. It's a tiara of lovingkindness and tender mercies. (Psalms 103:4) While doing so, he has redeemed our life from destruction. That is shouting ground, as the old folks would say! Oh, and to top it off, he says in Isaiah 28:5 *"In that day the Lord of hosts will be a crown of glory, and a diadem of beauty, to the remnant of his people."* What a mighty God we serve! We are in good hands along our journey.

Today, Christ is calling us unto betrothal as he desires a most intimate relationship with his people. When the journey has been long it is easy for our love to have grown cold without knowing it, like the Laodicean church in Revelation 3:15. At one time they started out hot for God, but along the way, for whatever reason, they had grown lukewarm. They received a stern warning from the Lord. He would vomit them from his mouth. They had to make changes in their relationship with the Lord and get back to status HOT. By this I mean they needed to have wholeheartedness unto God, have an undivided heart. That only comes by relationship and the laying down of one's life.

God is calling his church back to a deep personal intimate relationship with him in these end times. Unknowingly the church has relationships with meetings, conferences, community work, worship services and so forth and so on. I am not saying anything is wrong with the above mentioned activities, but you can do all those things without ever having a personal relationship with God. Those, my friend, are only external things. God deals with the internal. He is looking inside us, where he abides and gives us life. The trumpet is sounding today. Come out to Christ and forgo all the other things that distract. I said earlier we are on a journey unto a marriage. This is where God deals with us, and changes us as we allow him to.

I am certain some will not understand the message, but that's okay. As I have said, my mandate from God is to awaken the bride, sound the trumpet! I am not to worry about anything else. Christ is the great revealer of truth and the only one who can draw men and change hearts. Be blessed my friends, and may you say yes to the Lord and jump the broom today. Don't wait until after the big day. Do it now! Arise!

 *Two Shall Become One*

I am convinced that two becoming one in marriage is most challenging. One of the hardest things is to give up one's self. We all have desires, personal pet peeves and a certain way we do things. I mean, we were born from our spiritual parents Adam and Eve and we constantly have to battle the Adamic nature that is rival to the nature of Christ. Talking about a crucifixion! That's giving up my way of life for another. Christ was our prime example. In the garden of Gethsemane while facing crucifixion he cried, *"If possible, let this cup pass from me. But nevertheless, not my will but thy will be done."* (Luke 22:42) Christ had become one with his father and was yielded unto submission to his father. We all will and have faced these moments, some to triumph and some to failure. It's part of the journey that helps mature us. There will forever be only one life and that is Christ's life to be lived. It is not a dual life, not 'my life' and 'Christ's life.' We gave up our life when we accepted him. Or I should say, we should have.

In the book of Matthew 10:7-8

⁷For this cause shall a man leave his father and mother, and cleave to his wife;

⁸And they twain shall be one flesh: so then they are no more twain, but one flesh.

In order for the marriage to be in the perfect will of God, the man had to leave his parents and cleave to his wife and the two became one. This represents the one life we have in Christ, hidden in him. We cannot individually take along our old ways, habits of the former life, and expect them to fit in. Our old former life before we accepted Christ will not fit into our new life with him. Christ was very particular about his bride and protecting her.

All throughout the gospels we clearly see the relationship Christ had with his father. He always and only represented him. I must say, I have some growing to do. However, I'm on my may to becoming.

John 5:30-32

³⁰I can of mine own self do nothing: as I hear, I judge: and my judgment is just; because I seek not mine own will, but the will of the Father which hath sent me.

³¹If I bear witness of myself, my witness is not true.

³²There is another that beareth witness of me; and I know that the witness which he witnessed of me is true.

Simply amazing! Christ knew his whole entire existence was dependent on his father. He brought no attention to himself. He had become one with him. According to John 18:3 Christ's desire was for us to be one with the father. This speaks of union. The Bible concordance says union is becoming one in agreement, mind, spirit, will, affection, harmony and accord. This is exactly what we see exemplified in the life of Christ with his father. Marriage should not be any less as the two become one. One in heart, mind, will and intent. John 6:56 makes known to us that he who eats his flesh and drinks his blood is the one that has union with him. That means unless we appropriate his life, we have no life in us. We must stay virtually connected to the vine Christ. He that is joined unto the Lord is one Spirit with him. (I Corinthians 6:17)

Natural marriage was born from spiritual marriage. They are compatible with each other in reference to the two becoming one. Lives must be laid down for the other. The ring symbolized the never-ending covenant between the two. Christ is our never-ending covenant. He will always keep his word and honor it. Today let us reflect on our relationship with Christ. Are we in a separation status? A divorce status? A lukewarm status? Or just simply have walked away? I encourage you today that Christ is reaching out for you to come a little closer and lay down anything that may have come between you and him. He loves us with an everlasting love and is excited for the big day when we are forever eternally united to him by marriage, by becoming his bride. He paid the price, the dowry, for us.

May Christ blow on our hearts today and start a new fiery love that will ignite our passion for him. A fresh wind of his presence that will renew our strength and give us mental clarity of the day and time we are living and all that is required in this journey of the awakening of the bride. Hang in there, my brothers and sisters. We are in this thing together. Keep it moving. Remember the race is not given to the swift but to the one who endures to the end. Selah!

Journey

The word journey from its Latin meaning means a day's time. Do you know that a journey means to be in motion and not to stand still? The journey of life is full of twists and turns, ups and down, which is fine as long as we are not detoured from our destination. When I think of journeys I am reminded of the children of Israel and their journey from the wilderness into the Promised Land. As we travel along life's journey, we are confronted with ups and downs. You know the ups: friendship, graduations, fulfilling employment, a new baby, a promotion. But you know the downs too: sickness, death, depression, loss of a job, criticism. Regardless of the up or down, I must say its how we handle the situations that will determine how our journey ends. We cannot become paralyzed from the storms of life.

Let me briefly explain the children of Israel, as I am sure most know their story. God called Moses to deliver his people from their slavery from the Egyptians. The people were excited and had a bright outlook on the future but they could not imagine what the journey to freedom would require. In the book of Deuteronomy 1:2 Moses speaks of the journey from the wilderness which should have taken Israel less than two weeks to complete. Instead, because of the Israelite's unbelief and disobedience to God, the journey lasted forty years. The wilderness was an unfamiliar territory they had to tread on their journey. I would like to say it was so close and yet so far. This is because most died without reaching the Promised Land. Before it was over, they wanted to stone Moses because they were selfish and could not get their own way. How unfortunate they forgot what it was like to be a slave to Pharaoh. Can you believe they even spoke of turning back? That wanted to return to Egypt because they were not happy with their food or circumstances. WOW! I guess they forgot about what God had done for them on the journey. Though they were free on the outside, they were still prisoners inside.

In this section, let's examine our journey of life from a spiritual perspective and from the perspective of Christ. Some of you may feel as though you are just wandering through life, blowing in the wind. Getting up, rushing to work, waiting for the weekend. Sound familiar? Maybe you can't seem to find meaning in life or know why you were created by God. Let me help you on this leg of your journey today.

I Corinthians 1:9 says, *"God is faithful, by whom ye were called unto the fellowship of his Son Jesus Christ our Lord."* Along this journey of life, we are called to have fellowship with the Lord Jesus Christ. To have fellowship with someone, you have to get to know them by spending time with them. As we come to have fellowship with the Lord and come to be acquainted with him, he begins to unveil his plan for us on this journey called life. There is a scripture that says, *"He will order our steps in his word."* Psalms 119:33. I am a witness that this has made my life much easier. This is because I have not always been sure of where and how to walk in the journey called life. Should I take this job or not? Should I move here or not? Should I buy this or not? You get the picture.

It is understandable that we experience real life on this journey. Sometimes we make mistakes that seem impossible to rectify and the journey becomes frustrating and tiring. We may want to give up and pursue our own way. Let me encourage you today. You are not alone and you (or I) are not the first and won't be the last to mess things up. But there is always hope. Today I want to share a story of someone in the Bible who thought all was lost even after he had done what God told him to do. Sometimes God asks us to do things that he knows will challenge us and expose what's inside us. Trust me; God uses the journey as a process to prepare us for what's to come. I am sure you have heard that experience is the most effective teacher. I agree that Christ must be experienced to know him for yourself. Christ said it wasn't easy, but it would be worth it.

In the book of I Kings 19, under direction of the Lord, Elijah slaughtered all the prophets of Baal. He was threatened by the wicked Queen Jezebel who told him she was determined to take his life. Elijah became fearful and fled into the wilderness on a three-day journey and ended up under a tree. He was spiritually, emotionally and physically tired and drained and he just wanted to die. Elijah thought he was the only one who had not bowed to the wicked King. He was not. He was met by an angel who encouraged him to eat. I encourage you to read the whole story. As the story unfolds, it ends well, but not the way it seemed it would have turned out or even what he previously envisioned.

I understand how Elijah felt when he thought he was the only one that had not bowed. Walking with Christ is a lonely road. The Bible says *"The way is narrow and few will find it."* (Matthew 7:13) You might also be experiencing a challenging, fearful, emotionally and spiritually draining situation today along your awakening journey. *"Trust in the Lord with all your heart, and lean not on your own understanding."* (Proverbs 3:5-7) and *"Walk by faith, not by sight."* (II Corinthians 5:7) There is no way that any of us can see our way clearly God designed it for us to be able to trust him in every step we take.

In my own experience, over twelve years ago I fled to the wilderness. Or should say, God led me to the wilderness. There I found God for real and for myself. From the start of my journey, he told me "Just as fog covers a road and you can't see where you are going, that's the way I am leading you." Meaning I will lead and you will see when you get to the place I have meant for you to be. I can tell you it hasn't always been easy but this way has taught me to trust him and see his faithfulness. To this very day he has not changed this. I am forced to trust him in all things. Believe me, I have seen some pretty disturbing and fearful sights along my path. Only he could and can control the outcome. However, I am glad he has ordered my steps, which is why I have ended up where I am today. I am learning to walk by faith and not by sight. I love the scripture that says *"He knows the way that I take."* (Job 23:10.)

John 16:33 says that as we trust Christ, we will be provided with peace along our life journey. The same passage of scripture mentions that we will also face tribulation. We can have peace in the midst of our storms of life, brothers and sisters. II Timothy 2:3 tells us we have to endure hardness as a soldier. I would say knowing these things helps us to prepare along our journey which gives us the upper hand to win regardless of our situations. I always say to my friends "Life is tough and is not for punks"!

In conclusion, Matthew 24:13 states, *"He who endures to the end will be saved."* Now that's good news. All we have to do is endure and trust God to finish what he started. The wilderness you are experiencing today may be sickness, disease, or loneliness. Whatever it is, trust God and keep moving. Don't let distractions deter you from knowing Christ as your goal, savior, and redeemer. In the midst of your battle and journey think about what you are thinking about and if it is contrary to the word of God, put your mind back on the word. The word says *"I will keep him in complete peace whose mind is stayed on thee."* (Isaiah 26:3.) When we look around our world today it can be very troubling. Therefore, the only thing left is to keep our attention on him day by day as we proceed. It's time to awaken, my friend. Awaken to the Christ within. Enjoy the journey; I plan on it. Arise!

The Bride is Under Threat

I believe one of the greatest end time works of the enemy will be deception. Deception is not a bright shining light that draws attentions to itself. It can easily be hidden. It intertwines with truth; it presents itself as light and darkens understanding. Intertwined with deception are schemes, trickery, delusion and deceit. Delusion works through the door of good and says "This is okay. It's not hurting anyone". As my grandfather use to say "Might be good *to* you but not good *for* you. Amen! I have lived out that experience. The Lord gives a serious warning in II Thessalonians 2:10-11. I would suggest reading the whole chapter for the complete context of the message.

> *¹⁰"And with all deceivableness of unrighteousness in them that perish; because they received not the love of the truth, that they might be saved.*
>
> *¹¹And for this cause God shall send them strong delusion, that they should believe a lie"*

As the Lord who is the spirit of truth reveals himself in and through his word or a vessel, we must be careful that we not be one who received not the love of the truth. As we can see in scripture, because they did not receive the truth, Christ sent them strong delusion that they should believe a lie. Unfortunately, I am witnessing that scenario now, which breaks my heart and causes me to pray all the more for the body of Christ as well as myself. When one is deceived, they are incapable of ever receiving the truth. Deception is like a boxer who backs his opponent into a corner and keeps him from ever getting out and off the ropes of the delusions.

I remember years ago when the Lord brought me out to himself. He directed me to throw out a lot of what I had been taught over the years, He dissected things I had been taught and separated the truth from an error. At that time, I was in a very vulnerable state as this was all new to me, but I knew it was truth that I had to accept. I would encourage and caution each reader to not always be so quick to throw out information or truth you may not readily understand. Perhaps, it could very well be the Lord opening up the eyes of your understanding to truth that may need to be revealed or even a lie that may need to be uncovered because it is hidden. A good example is Numbers 22. Balaam the servant of the Lord would not obey the Lord. God used a donkey, yes, a talking donkey, to not only talk but to see the Angel standing in the road Balaam himself could not see. Balaam still would not listen. I encourage you to read the complete story for yourself. It's very insightful. God is very gracious as I am reminded of Abram. Remember, he had problems grasping the promise when the Lord told him that he would have a child. In Genesis chapter 15 Abram and Sarai were childless and the Lord told him he would have an heir coming from his body. This seemed like an impossibility to Abram. I understand why he might have had a hard time wrapping around his head around the truth of what the Lord was saying. The Lord went as far as to make a covenant with Abram to honor his word. What a mighty God we serve. But brothers and sisters sometimes the Lord does not always do that and we have to walk it out by faith and trust him, the truth that he is. Christ is our protection from deception.

One of the most unfathomable things for me to comprehend is how Lucifer was able to deceive one-third of the angels to join in with him to try and overthrow God their creator. They lived, worshiped, and danced around the throne of God. They knew God and were known by him, yet these angels were deceived. This is so stupendous to me. Lucifer's name in Hebrew means Day Star. A star stands out because of its brightness. It stands to reason he was called Lucifer.

II Corinthians 11:14

14And no marvel; for Satan himself is transformed into an angel of light. After the fall and being kicked out of heaven his brightness became defiled.

Ezekiel 28:7

7Behold, therefore I will bring strangers upon thee, the terrible of the nations: and they shall draw their swords against the beauty of thy wisdom, and they shall defile thy brightness.

Our remedy to steer from delusion and deception is having a deep intimate, personal relationship with Christ. John 15 tells us Christ is the true vine. We must abide in him and bring forth fruit or we are cast away to wither and die. Deception and delusion definitely will cause us to come to no good end. Oh! But when we stay vitally connected to the vine Christ, we live in and through him and his life flows through us. He is wisdom; he is understanding. We are able to see clearly what is true light and truth. His light of truth keeps us from a darkened understanding which is lies and deception. John 16:13 says *"When the spirit of truth comes, he will guide you into all the truth."* The blessed Holy Spirit our helper will help us. We must be careful to not grieve him. He is so precious and sensitive.

Ephesians 1:18 declares,

18The eyes of your understanding being enlightened; that ye may know what is the hope of his calling, and what the riches of the glory of his inheritance in the saints. The eyes of our understanding have been brightened with divine illumination.

How many know the illumination of light that is Christ? He shines a spotlight on Satan and his defiled light of deception which causes real damage to the bride. Satan's strategy is to lead the bride away from Christ our Bridegroom. He is an imposter that tries to duplicate the voice of Christ. Let us be aware of the enemies' devices.

II Corinthians 2:11

¹¹Lest Satan should get an advantage of us: for we are not ignorant of his devices.

Along my journey I have noticed the enemy thrives on ignorance. It is easy to be robbed if you are ignorant or unwarily not in the know. Just because I was not aware of something or simply did not know something, such as information that could have been useful to me, it did not stop the enemy from stealing or attacking me. He thrives on our ignorance; it's a part of his game. We must wake up if we are not aware of the hidden war we are in every day. The Devil is a ruthless, vicious enemy who hates Christ and the Christ in us. He wants to be worshiped and called Lord. Let us awaken and put on the armor of light.

Romans 13:12

¹²The night is far spent, the day is at hand: let us therefore cast off the works of darkness, and let us put on the armor of light.

I also believe another major threat to the bride is distractions. Remember the parable of the great banquet, the wedding feast in Matthew 22:1-5. Christ first sent his servants to invite a certain group and they did not respond. Again, he sent his servants to invite another group to come but the scripture said they made light of it. Why? To make light of something is to not count it important. As the Lord enlightened my understanding, I found a hidden message. It is this: everyday distraction can be our Kryptonite, which is a weakness of some sort.

In the parable, one group of people went their way for some reason, distracted by something they thought at the time needed immediate attention. The other one went to his business. It looks like they were distracted. The meaning of distraction from Oxford Languages is a thing that prevents someone from giving full attention to something else. Here we see that's exactly what happened. In the eyes of the King, they made light of the invitation. It was ignored.

The Lord directed me to look at this passage again from a different point of my understanding. I can see how easy it is to miss the will of God if we don't stop, look, and listen to him. I understand more clearly when he says in his word *"My thoughts and ways are higher than your thoughts and ways."* (Isaiah 55:8-9)

Proverbs tells in 14:12

12 There is a way which seemeth right unto a man, but the end thereof are the ways of death.

A way is a course of action or path. On our path or journey with the Lord, we must be totally surrendered to his way and not our own. Believe me, I know that's easier said than done. But with Christ and if we allow him, he will navigate us. He is the way through these dark days. He leads us and shows us the way around the tricks of the enemy. May we only see as the Lamb of God sees, go only where he goes and say only what he says.

It is in Christ we live move and have our being. (Acts 17:8) He is the light that overcomes darkness. He is the defender of his bride. May he arise within us. Amen! So be it. Can you hear the trumpet sounding?

The Husbandman

The day and time have come that the church must realize she is the Bride of Christ if she makes herself ready. Her Bridal Identity must be embraced in order to make preparations. After talking and listening to people, my observation and general consensus is that very few are aware of the Bridal call to become the bride without spot, wrinkle, blemish or any such thing. If we are to be prepared to meet and marry our Husbandman Christ our story is not quite like Cinderella who had only a few hours to prepare. Our preparation requires daily journey with the Lord.

One day, my cousin and I were sharing about the things of God and she said "You know I never hear much preached about the church having a bridal relationship with the Lord." I agree, but today is a day of awakening to the fact the church is meant to become a Glorious Bride without spot or wrinkle or any such thing. (Ephesians 5:27). That, my friends, takes time. To mature in Christ and allow his life in us to grow is not accomplished overnight. His life in us started out as a seed when we accepted him but he must be allowed to bloom and grow and increase in us. His life and nature must radiate in and through us in his nature and character, the fruit of his vine. We started out on milk but as the word says we must move on to meat and grow up in him in all things (I Peter 2:2). As we eat of the Lord, yielded and allowing his correction and chastening in our lives, we move on to maturity to become sons and daughters of God.

When I started out on this journey with the Lord, he instructed me to keep it simple. "Don't out-think the room, Rochelle." In the past I was notorious for make things more complicated than they needed to be. He reminded me he is within and I must let him be who he is. In walking with the Lord, I have come to learn how he deals with me. In the simplest ways, he has expressed who he is. That helps me understand in very simplistic and general ways. Under his direction it has been my instruction from him to pen not only this book but also the previous one so simple that anyone can understand. I recall how he spoke in parables to his disciples. So, I in turn say to you 'don't out-think the room' as you journey to know this God. If you allow him in, let him grow, he will come out in all of his nature. He will be wisdom when you need it, kindness, support and your great teacher, the Holy Spirit. So let us continue to take this journey of awakening and becoming all God intends us to become. We have a big day coming.

When you contemplate on Christ the Vinedresser what comes to mind? As I prayed and pondered over this thought I heard the Lord say, "I dress the bride" I thought oh, okay. That's right, simple Ugh? He is the true vine, the Husbandman. (John 15) "I prune the bride; I dress the bride." The father, the Husbandman is the vinedresser. Marriage is about union with Christ. We journey in union and communion being vitally connected to the vine and because of that connection, we bear fruit. The Vinedresser will purge us, or prune us, so that we may bear more and more glorious fruit. Prune means to cleanse and purify. It is the Vinedresser's job to work and till the garden of our hearts. He will remove the weeds of distraction, selfishness and so much more that crowds our hearts. We can be sure the gardener will overturn and disrupt all spiritual insects of flesh and self that hinder his garden.

God told Adam and Eve to tend to the garden, dress and keep it. Seeds have to be sown and cultivated for a beautiful garden to come forth. So, we must ask ourselves, "What am I sowing? Am I sowing to the flesh or to the spirit?" Be sure, we will get exactly what we sow.

For the beautiful Bride to come forth to be arrayed in all of her glory we must stay vitally connected to the source of our life, Christ. Apart from him we can do nothing. (I Corinthians 6:1). He that is joined unto the Lord is one Spirit with him, vitally connected to the vine. Christ's aim is to present to his father a glorious church. (Ephesians 5:27) *"That he might present it to himself a glorious church, not having spot, or wrinkle, or any such thing; but that it should be holy and without blemish."* Without spot means without fault or blemish. I am reminded when Jesus was on trial see (Luke 23:1-44) and they brought him to Pilate and he said *"I find no fault in him."* And in *John 14:30 "The Lord said the prince of this world cometh and find nothing in me."* These are amazing examples for the bride to be found without spot or any defilement. That's what the journey is all about. We come to know Christ and learn to walk with him closely and most intimately. The scripture went on to say the bride must be without wrinkle, spiritual defect or flawed, but rather she must be holy, set apart, scared and blameless, meaning without blemish. We know this type of maturing in our walk with the Lord takes time and preparation. How we live each day matters.

In Galatians 5:22-25 we see the fruit are the virtues and life of Christ that will dress the bride. She will be dressed with the nature of the Vinedresser. Christ's nature is the fruit of the Spirit. His bride will be dressed in glory and represent the life of Christ.

Be assured and aware, pruning and remaining connected to the vine will be necessary for this glorious fruit to increases more and more. Though the pruning process is never comfortable or easy, don't despise the temperature of the test. The fiery trials are a part of the process. The process is not for our destruction but for our construction. Our fruit must be squeezed. Resistance is necessary for growth and transition. There will be no spiritual genetic engineering. We will have to journey, fight and go through the complete process as we are being transformed. But on an encouraging note, remember

II Corinthians 4:17 NLT

For our present troubles are small and won't last very long. Yet they produce for us a glory that vastly outweighs them and will last forever.

Finally through it all let us look at the end results.

Revelations 19:7-8

"Let us rejoice and be glad and give Him the glory. For the marriage of the Lamb has come, and His bride has made herself ready. She was given clothing of fine linen, bright and pure. For the fine linen she wears is the righteous acts of the saints".

What a beautiful ending! I encourage you to enjoy the journey of awakening to become all God would have you be. Let us stay the course and follow the Lamb wherever he goes.

Are You Asleep?

I remember when I was in high school, I got tired of always not having any extra money to do anything. I came from a blended family and had five other siblings. We were not well off and did well to have lunch money. One day I came to the conclusion that I needed to get me a part-time job and have my own money. I found a weekend job working for a hospital in the kitchen. The only thing I did not like was it was from 5am to 2pm Saturday and Sunday. My friends and I loved to party and stay out all night long, even though I knew I had to be at work at 5am. Of course, I always stayed out too late and in most cases only was able to sleep a couple of hours. In the break room there was a small leather love seat and between every break I could squeeze in I would go to that break room and try to catch a snooze. How many know once you snooze it's so hard to wake up? I was asleep when I should have been working and it put me behind in most cases. It was just so hard to wake up because I was tired and sleep deprived.

As we look forward to our great wedding day approaching, our final reuniting with the Lord, are we too sleeping as I was when we should be working unto preparation? I'm sure you are familiar with the story of Jesus final hours in the garden of Gethsemane before being crucified. Let take a look at the passage to refresh our memories. For some this may be new.

Mark 14:32

³²And they came to a place which was named Gethsemane: and he saith to his disciples, Sit ye here, while I shall pray.

³³And he taketh with him Peter and James and John, and began to be sore amazed, and to be very heavy;

³⁴And saith unto them, My soul is exceeding sorrowful unto death: tarry ye here, and watch.

³⁵And he went forward a little, and fell on the ground, and prayed that, if it were possible, the hour might pass from him.

³⁶And he said, Abba, Father, all things are possible unto thee; take away this cup from me: nevertheless not what I will, but what thou wilt.

³⁷And he cometh, and findeth them sleeping, and saith unto Peter, Simon, sleepest thou? couldest not thou watch one hour?

³⁸Watch ye and pray, lest ye enter into temptation. The spirit truly is ready, but the flesh is weak.

³⁹And again he went away, and prayed, and spake the same words.

⁴⁰And when he returned, he found them asleep again, (for their eyes were heavy,) neither wist they what to answer him.

⁴¹And he cometh the third time, and saith unto them, Sleep on now, and take your rest: it is enough, the hour is come; behold, the Son of man is betrayed into the hands of sinners.

⁴²Rise up, let us go; lo, he that betrayeth me is at hand.

We are living in a day and time we cannot afford to be asleep. With all that is going on in the world and the nations of the earth, we need to awaken! Did you know we, the church, the bride, are the solution? Christ arising in us as light will overtake the darkness. We must be praying and not sleeping as the Lord told his disciples. Jesus knew his hour of testing was upon him and asked his disciples to pray also.

I am sure you know and have experienced that before a great victory there is always a great trial. That's what makes victory so sweet when you overcome. I remember some of the old church mothers used to say when they see victory arising "It's all over but the shouting!" LOL! Right! Christ's great trial was Gethsemane. The Hebrew meaning of the word is garden, oil press. It is common knowledge the olive press is where olives are brought to be pressed and turned into olive oil. In the olive press extreme pressure is applied. Our Savior endured the pressure of Gethsemane. Jesus had to go through Gethsemane in order to return back to his father and receive his former glory. But he first had to redeem us man. Thank you Jesus!

What if Christ would have decided not to pray and like his disciples had slept through a defining moment? We would not be here. Are you asleep? Am I asleep? *"Watch ye and pray lest yet enter into temptation. The Spirit truly is willing but the flesh is weak."* (Mark 14:38) Yep, that flesh, that old Adamic nature, will give you a run for your money. Who better knew than the Apostle Paul?

Romans 7:14-24

14For we know that the law is spiritual: but I am carnal, sold under sin.

15For that which I do I allow not: for what I would, that do I not; but what I hate, that do I.

16If then I do that which I would not, I consent unto the law that it is good.

17Now then it is no more I that do it, but sin that dwelleth in me.

18For I know that in me (that is, in my flesh,) dwelleth no good thing: for to will is present with me; but how to perform that which is good I find not.

19For the good that I would I do not: but the evil which I would not, that I do.

²⁰Now if I do that I would not, it is no more I that do it, but sin that dwelleth in me.

²¹I find then a law, that, when I would do good, evil is present with me.

²²For I delight in the law of God after the inward man:

²³But I see another law in my members, warring against the law of my mind, and bringing me into captivity to the law of sin which is in my members.

²⁴O wretched man that I am! who shall deliver me from the body of this death?

This passage of scripture speaks volumes! Every day is a battle and a fight. I too, like Paul, do things I do not want at times. But the victory comes by continuing to be submitted to Christ and allowing the growth and increase of his life in me and you. The passage is simply the reality of life and journeying with Christ. Jesus saw and knew of the battle and told the disciples from the get-go to watch and pray. He knew how weak their flesh was and his also because he was both son of man and son of God. After Jesus told them to watch and pray, he found them asleep on two more occasions. On the third occasion he told them to take their rest as the hour had come for the son of man to be betrayed unto the hands of sinners. I can only imagine coming out of a deep sleep from being so tired and to hear words like that.

In all of my writings and just fellowshipping with others I will always and forever push the importance of a deep personal intimate relationship with Christ. In most cases, just like Jesus, you will more than likely end up standing alone. The narrow road is never crowded because there's a price that must be paid. I believe Jesus asked the disciples to pray not only for him or with him but also for themselves because he knew what they all were about to face. Jesus knew his dark hour of testing; his Gethsemane moment had come. He stood alone to do the will of his father even though he said "Father, if possible, let this cup pass from me but nevertheless not my will but they will be done."

(Luke 22:42)

If chance and circumstance cause us to stand alone on our journey of awakening with Christ, will you or I be ready? I know it's not easy though it will be worth it. Jesus is called our PERSONAL Lord and savior. What he may require of you he may not require of others because he may have something specific for you to do along your journey. Peter, James, and John, who were asked to pray with Jesus in the garden, had much to do after Christ returned to heaven. Jesus knew that their role in the years ahead would require a close relationship with the Savior. All twelve of the disciples were not with Christ in the garden, yet all were preparing for their roles in spreading the gospel. When walking with Christ we take a risk. In general, we all want to be liked by everyone, accepted, understood, and loved. Unfortunately, that's just not reality; it wasn't for Jesus and it won't be for us. It wasn't for the disciples either. They faced persecution and death because of their calling. Walking with Christ can be a lonely and difficult road. I have encountered this along my journey of walking with Christ and going after him. I have and continue to come to grips with this issue and realize to walk with Christ is a lonely journey. Misunderstandings along with being on the outside looking in is a part of it. We all have our personal Gethsemane and we to must watch and pray. No time for sleeping; the hour is late.

Gethsemane is where the rubber meets the road. As I said, we all, like Christ, have a personal Gethsemane. I like to call it where we meet Shock & Awe moments. Where we become faced with decisions that cause us to, like Christ, be deeply troubled in soul. We anguish because Christ is asking of us something so great that's far beyond our ability to accomplish, let alone see at all. The price is great. This is the moment where it's 'my will' or 'thy will Lord be done.' It's a crossroads. A crossroads is a critical point where a decision must be made. Usually, our decisions will have an affect other people and we tend to have that in mind, but the Lord is only waiting for "not my will." Yes, it is a risk, a challenge and submission. But remember, Christ always has our best interest at heart.

As in the book of Revelation, Christ stands at the door of our hearts and knocks. Who will come out to him to be his Bride? It takes time and preparation. Who is willing to go, even though you may have to go it alone? Who is willing to take up their cross daily and follow Christ? Who is willing to recommit in their relationship with Christ today? Is there a prodigal son or daughter who needs to come home and return back to Christ today? Are you waking up out of your sleep? Can you hear the sounding of the trumpet? It's time to watch and pray. The bridegroom is standing at the door waiting and ready. Today is the day of salvation. If any man hears his voice and opens the door and he will come in and sup with you. If you said yes Lord, it's all over but the shouting! Awaken Oh Bride.

A Worthy Bride

Many times, before arising as I lie in my bed and see the beautiful bright sun shining through my window, I can't help but think about the goodness of God. Especially when I begin to reminiscence over my life before Christ, the BC days. I find myself in many characters of the Bible. I mean, nothing is new under the sun. We know sin will never be new and outdated until Christ returns for his Bride. We see all thoughout scriptures the stories of life in general, the ups and downs, the highs and low in the matriarchs and patriarchs lives as they literally walked with Christ. I am sure there were days they made such a mess of things that they thought 'I am so undone and unworthy because of the stupid stuff I do' and yet Christ remains faithful. I know I have felt that way many times, but oh! All though-out the scriptures I see Christ the loving and forgiving God that he is allows his love to trump my shortcomings. He is willing and able to help me overcome my weaknesses and the bride's.

I am reminded of the adulterous women in John chapter eight. Though I have never married, like her I've found myself in situations where others would cast stones. My accusers had their own opinionated law of what is good and acceptable in their eyes. Like the scribes and Pharisees, they would rather cast stones from their opinion and decide what would be a just reward for someone's stupidity or an honest mistake. But God! In examination of the scripture John 8:1-11 NLT

8Jesus returned to the Mount of Olives,²but early the next morning he was back again at the Temple. A crowd soon gathered, and he sat down and taught them.³As he was speaking, the teachers of religious law and the Pharisees brought a woman who had been caught in the act of adultery. They put her in front of the crowd.

⁴"Teacher," they said to Jesus, "this woman was caught in the act of adultery.⁵The law of Moses says to stone her. What do you say?"

⁶They were trying to trap him into saying something they could use against him, but Jesus stooped down and wrote in the dust with his finger.⁷They kept demanding an answer, so he stood up again and said, "All right, but let the one who has never sinned throw the first stone!"⁸Then he stooped down again and wrote in the dust.

⁹When the accusers heard this, they slipped away one by one, beginning with the oldest, until only Jesus was left in the middle of the crowd with the woman.¹⁰Then Jesus stood up again and said to the woman, "Where are your accusers? Didn't even one of them condemn you?"

¹¹"No, Lord," she said.

And Jesus said, "Neither do I. Go and sin no more."

I love it! Right in the face of her accusers Jesus said *"He who is without sin, let him cast the first stone."* BOOM! All the accusers had no choice but to put down their stones and slip away, more than likely with a crushed ego. I can only envision how unworthy the women must have felt. But God! Regardless of what you or I have done, we have been made worthy through Christ. He has such a forgiving and overwhelming love for us! Perhaps you are feeling you have just blown it because of sin and stupid decisions. Lift up your head! Jesus is walking by and coming your way. Repent! And as he told the women, "Go and sin no more." Do not make sin your lifestyle. Yes, we all make mistakes. There is a difference between willful sinning and making a mistake. Know the difference! God hates sin and we should too. After all, that is why he had to go to the cross and die, because of our sins. May we honor him in our living daily.

Let's look at one more example, the women with the issue of blood in Matthew 9:20-22. The women had an issue of blood for twelve long years and spent all she had hoping for a cure. Yet she was none better but rather grew worse. I no doubt believe at times she was depressed and hopeless, disappointed because of the hand life had dealt her. When she heard Jesus coming, she thrust her way through the throngs of people. When she came up behind Jesus she touched his garment. Because of her faith everything changed. I can only visualize the cold hard stares of the others as they wondered, "What are you doing?" As though she was not worthy to be amongst the crowd! Oh, I'm sure you have found yourself in that type of situation, be it on your job, amongst friend or foe. When she touched his clothes, he said, "Who touched my clothes?" (John 7:31-34) The disciples were a little confused seeing all the people pushing through the crowd and he asked who touched him? But Christ knew because virtue left his body. The women, knowing what she had done, humbled herself before the Lord in fear and told him the truth. Jesus said, "Daughter thy faith has made thee whole." It is important, my friend, where we place our trust. She could have easily placed her faith in herself and others but no, she placed her faith in Christ. That is where our faith must be against all odds. Believe me; I am sure most of us are facing many circumstances against all odds. That is in the natural. But we know God is faithful. The unseen realm is more real than the seen realm. Let us rise up and move forward toward Christ. How about that?

Let us move on to the heart of the teaching, which is found in the book of Hosea. This is one of many beautiful love stories and shows the length Christ will go to for his bride regardless of her state because he loves her passionately. Marriage is all about a union of love. When I hear the word marriage, I think of two people so madly in love with one another, the excitement of spending your live with someone and living happily ever after. I would have to believe a person would be insane or blinded by love to marry someone that is promiscuous. This is the story of Hosea and Gomer. I would encourage you to read and study the whole story for complete context and understanding. Due to the sake of time, I will briefly hit certain points of importance. Remember Proverbs 25:2 *"It's the glory of God to conceal a thing and the honor of kings to search it out."* That means we are to study the word for ourselves. The marriage of Hosea and Gomer was full of betrayal, conflict, pain, passion, and what I like to call trauma drama. The book of Hosea portrays a picture of Israel, God's people, and their idolatry and unfaithfulness to their covenant with God. God, knowing Gomer was a prostitute, a promiscuous woman, asks Hosea to marry her to exemplify how much he loved her even in her unfaithfulness and one-sided love. Gomer's marital infidelity is a picture of Israel's idolatry and unfaithfulness to its covenant with God.

I can't image what it was for Hosea and the father's heart to be broken by infidelity and a cold love. God's love toward his bride was ceaseless as he chased after her all at the same time drawing her with his love. Through Hosea, God portrayed love and forgiveness. God's love for Israel was loyal because he was covenanted with her. He remains faithful even when we are not. That is covenant. Hosea 11:1-10

> *¹When Israel was a child, then I loved him, and called my son out of Egypt.*
>
> *²As they called them, so they went from them: they sacrificed unto Balaam, and burned incense to graven images.*
>
> *³I taught Ephraim also to go, taking them by their arms; but they knew not that I healed them.*
>
> *⁴I drew them with cords of a man, with bands of love: and I was to them as they that take off the yoke on their jaws, and I laid meat unto them.*
>
> *⁵He shall not return into the land of Egypt, and the Assyrian shall be his king, because they refused to return.*

⁶And the sword shall abide on his cities, and shall consume his branches, and devour them, because of their own counsels.

⁷And my people are bent to backsliding from me: though they called them to the most High, none at all would exalt him.

⁸How shall I give thee up, Ephraim? how shall I deliver thee, Israel? how shall I make thee as Admah? how shall I set thee as Zeboim? mine heart is turned within me, my repenting's are kindled together.

⁹I will not execute the fierceness of mine anger, I will not return to destroy Ephraim: for I am God, and not man; the Holy One in the midst of thee: and I will not enter into the city.

¹⁰They shall walk after theLord: he shall roar like a lion: when he shall roar, then the children shall tremble from the west.

Absolutely beautiful! God drew them with bands of love! Amazing! What a loving, forgiving God we serve!

I'm sure by now you get the just of this story and journal. Could it be that we too have become Gomer in our idolatry toward God? Did we start with God by laying our lives down but have picked them up and started serving other lovers like Gomar did? What do I mean by other lovers? I mean things that take the place of God in our hearts where he should be. What do I serve more than him, who and what do I give my time to if not God? Do I even have time for him at all? Do I wear his name but not his life or nature? Can others tell that I belong to him and him alone? These questions are food for thought and consideration. We cannot be in a relationship with Christ and are never engaged by him or give him ourselves. God has showed us how far he will go to reach us because he loves us so much. He demonstrated this great love when he sent his only son to die for our sins. *"While we were yet sinners, Christ died for us."* (Romans 5:8) Walking with God and being a Christian is more than just the name. It is a lifestyle of union and relationship. Today the Lord is reaching out to his bride drawing her with cords of love. Let today be a new day of returning back to our first love that we may make ourselves ready to meet him and allow him to make us ready. I will say it a thousand times; it's a journey of growing a relationship with Christ by daily walking with him.

Today let us view the story from God's position. How would any of us feel if that was our living reality? For some it could possibly be? It has always stood out to me in the scripture when the Lord speaks of adultery in Matthew chapter five. Sexual immorality is grounds for divorce. Sexual immorality is something that cuts deep and is very hurtful. The Lord understood and made a way of escape if that's what a person chooses to do. So, when I look at it from that standpoint I must stop, pause and consider. "Am I hurting the Lord who I am covenanted with because I still choose to live my own life as though I am my own and never consider the Lord who I am covenanted with?" It's a heavy topic but must be considered. There are questions in my life that must be addressed if I am to move on with the Lord to becoming a bride made ready. I want to be his worthy bride. Don't you?

Hosea 10:12

¹²Sow to yourselves in righteousness, reap in mercy; break up your fallow ground: for it is time to seek the Lord, till he come and rain righteousness upon you.

It's time to seek the Lord and he will come. Know today how much your God loves you. He will go to the ends of the earth for you because you are his precious possession. You are his worthy bride and he stands at the door to dress you in beautiful garments. Selah!

The Vinedresser

I believe the time has come for the church to have an awareness that she is the Bride of Christ. Her Bridal Identity must be embraced in order to make preparations. And time is running out. The signs are all around, but few are aware; few are even looking. Let's wake up, people!

After conversing and listening to people, my observation has been that very few are aware of the Bridal call. Most people haven't considered that Christ wants us to become the bride without spot, wrinkle or any such thing. If we are to be prepared to meet and marry our Husbandman Christ, our preparation requires daily journey with the Lord. We must be on this journey of relationship to become deeply and intimately acquainted with Christ. I often wonder "If I am one day planning on going to heaven to live forever, what reason am I going?" I know God the Father resides there and I will be with him so why would I think I don't need to know him while down here on earth? It's really ludicrous when I think about it.

As I stated in an earlier chapter, we don't hear much about the bride of Christ in our church services these days. Think about it. Has this topic been covered, or even briefly mentioned, in sermons or teachings you have heard? And as far as preparation and becoming a glorious Bride without spot or wrinkle or any such thing, (Ephesians 5:27) I'm honestly not recalling any discussion.

Friends, we are running out of time. Today is a day of awakening to the fact that the church is meant to be the bride of Christ, and we need to get ready *now*. We can't wait till the last minute to make our preparations. My friends, it requires time to mature in Christ.

When we accepted him as our personal Lord and Savior we were baby Christians. As the word saturated our hearts and minds, we moved toward a deeper relationship with Jesus. But we can't allow ourselves to remain in one place. We must keep maturing in Christ, allowing him to change and purify us. He wants his bride to be totally committed to him. As I've said before and will say again, that requires a daily fellowship and a covenant of self-sacrifice. As it says in I Peter 2:2, *"As newborn babes, desire the sincere milk of the word, that ye may grow thereby."* As we eat of the Lord by reading and studying his word, as we yield and allow his correction and chastening in our lives, we move on to maturity to become sons and daughters of God.

I want to give caution that as we journey with the Lord from time to time, we need to stop and take check of our spiritual progress. We cannot remain the same. Change is part of maturity. I am sure you will hear me make that statement all throughout this journal. If you stop and think, even in the natural world the medical pediatric association has a system of measurement called Ages and Stages. Ages and Stages are developmental milestones for babies and children. Milestones serve as behavioral and physical checkpoints. Physicians look for weekly and monthly check points for development. Milestone checks allow us to stay ahead of the curve. In the event growth is not progressing properly, the checkpoints help to alert us to the possible problem. For the Body of Christ, the Bride of Christ it is no different. Christ must and should be increasing in us as we go from a baby Christian unto a full mature Christian. I must know and be honest with myself. If I am the same person I was when I first accepted Christ, something has happened and I have missed some spiritual milestones. This must be corrected in order that I may go on to become a spiritual man in full maturity. This is an area the Lord wants me to make plain and sound the trumpet on. So many in the body of Christ are yet remaining the same. Profession of faith in Christ and declaring the name 'Christian' require change and growth. Let us awaken and be honest with ourselves. We have to desire a closer, intimate relationship with Christ so that we may go on and become the beautiful bride Christ intends us to become. He will draw us to himself, but we must be willing to move closer and closer to him. Selah.

For the beautiful Bride to come forth and be arrayed in all of her glory we must stay vitally connected to the source of our life, Christ. *Apart from him we can do nothing.* (I Corinthians 6:17) He that is joined unto the Lord is one Spirit with him, vitally connected to the vine.

In Galatians 5:22-25 we see that Christ's bride will be dressed with the nature of the Vinedresser. Christ's nature will be reflected in the fruits of the Spirit. The bride is to be dressed in glory as the representation of Christ's life dwelling within.

I'm sure you have heard 'gifts are free and given but fruit is grown.' The fruits of the spirit grow through process and overtime. Weeding and pruning, though unpleasant, are necessary. On a encouraging note remember that in the end, they produce for us a glory that vastly outweighs will last forever. I love that saying 'the pain is worth the gain.' Be encouraged my friends. *Greater is he that is in us than he that is in the world.* (I John 4:4)

Finally, through it all look at the end Revelation 19:7-8

"Let's rejoice and be glad and give the glory to Him, because the marriage of the Lamb has come, and His bride has prepared herself."

Amen!

Separation Unto Preparation

I recall the days when I was a teenager and looked forward to watching the Miss Universe Pageant. I love fashion and was always excited to see all the ladies from the many different countries model their dresses and showcase their talent. The excitement they were exuberating was so evident it was as though it came through the TV screen right into my living room! I kept my fingers crossed for the one I hoped would win. I can only imagine the depth of the preparation it took to get ready for the big day and the stage runway. In the end only one would be chosen and crowned Miss Universe.

While researching on the pageant website I found there are over 190 nations of women that participate. Only the most beautiful and talented individuals will qualify. There are two preliminary competitions to determine who will move along and be chosen in the final competition. All competitors must have a talent, great interviewing skills and be prepared for a lot of rehearsals for the big day. I no doubt believe the candidates had to prepare by choosing a great wardrobe, especially the gown which seems to be the signature attire for the pageant. I know my main focal point of interest was the gowns. I loved seeing their beauty and distinction. I am certain the contestants were very cautious about what they ate and were on a strict diet. They had great hair stylists and makeup artists. Preparation is very challenging but necessary for the chance to be crowned Miss Universe.

In some sense and similarities, the Miss Universe Pageant reminds me of the Bible story Esther. This is one of my favorite books in the Bible. She was in a similar situation in reference to being crowned as Queen and she too had to go through a process and purification. Her story was tied to saving her nation and people. Her being crowned as Queen hinged on her being chosen by the King. I'm sure most of you are familiar with her story in the book of Esther. I will not go into great detail in this journal but will as we move further along in the book. My primary emphasis for this journal deals with the process of preparation and our preparation in reference to meeting the King of Kings. In preparation there will first be an internal preparation that will affect the external preparation. The candidates for the Miss Universe Pageant first off needed to have confidence in themselves. They had to believe they were up for the task amongst so many other beautiful and talented women. They had to obviously love what they were doing as it would be revealed though their smiles. One thing I remember the judges always repeated was to smile and show that you are having fun. The external process of preparation is what I mention earlier about the wardrobe and all the other details.

Esther was an orphan. Her parents had died when she was very young. She resided with her cousin Mordecai who raised her. Starting out, her external circumstances were not great, but she was beautiful inside and out. Internally, her heart is what won it for her. She was a woman who loved her God and her people. Her love prepared her for her task ahead to be crowned Queen. Once she was chosen to be a queen candidate, she had to endure much preparation to have a chance at becoming queen. Esther and the other beautiful girls were rounded up to be taken for twelve months of beauty treatments before being brought before the king. The preparation consisted of six months of oil and myrrh and six months of sweet ardors. Myrrh as cited in the Ultimate Bible Dictionary as an aromatic resin used as a perfume. Myrrh and cassia are spices that were used as scared oils described in Exodus 30:23-24

Take thou also unto thee principal spices, of pure myrrh five hundred shekels, and of sweet cinnamon half so much, even two hundred and fifty shekels, and of sweet calamus two hundred and fifty shekels.

Myrrh also was used for perfuming clothe and beds also as stated Proverbs 7:17 *I have perfumed my bed with myrrh, aloes, and cinnamon.* I must say I love perfume and my house filled with the aroma of a beautiful scent. Myrrh is an oil that was also used by priests in the temple. Most beautiful and unique about Myrrh was it was offered as a gift to the baby Jesus when he was born in a manger.(Matthew 2:11) *"They bowed down and worship him and opened their treasure chest with gifts of gold and frankincense along with myrrh."* Looks like to me in their day they took preparation seriously. And just think - Esther was preparing to go before an earthly king. We are preparing to stand before the heavenly eternal king, Jesus Christ. Selah!

Let us focus on the preparation in our day from the word of God. Just as the king in Esther's day desired all beautiful women and virgins, Christ's bride will be a virgin because she is pure, spotless, and without blemish. It is no different for us. We must have on the right garments. That's what preparation is all about - getting the right garment, making changes if necessary. In the natural realm things, a bride may need a seamstress to make alterations on her clothing so that everything fits properly on her big day.

Apostle Paul in I Thessalonians 5:23-24 AMP

²³*Now may the God of peace Himself sanctify you through and through [that is, separate you from profane and vulgar things, make you pure and whole and undamaged—consecrated to Him—set apart for His purpose]; and may your spirit and soul and body be kept complete and [be found] blameless at the coming of our Lord Jesus Christ.*

²⁴*Faithful and absolutely trustworthy is He who is calling you [to Himself for your salvation], and He will do it [He will fulfill His call by making you holy, guarding you, watching over you, and protecting you as His own].*

What a beautiful encouraging passage of scripture. It looks like Christ in us means he doeth the work as he calls us to himself. Our part is to give him consent and submit to his will and his way. We must make sure our spirit, soul and body are kept blameless as we prepare and wait for him.

One scripture I believe that will sum it all up this journal is Romans 13:14 AMP

> *14But clothe yourselves with the Lord Jesus Christ, and make no provision for [nor even think about gratifying] the flesh in regard to to it's improper desires.*

All I can say is "My God!" when I read that passage of scripture. Clothe yourself with the Lord. We allow his life to be reproduced through us, all that he is, and his nature becomes our own.

Galatians 5:22

> *22But the fruit of the Spirit is love, joy, peace, forbearance, kindness, goodness, faithfulness,*
>
> *23gentleness and self-control. Against such things there is no law.*

If we allow ourselves to be clothed with Christ, our spirits will exude all that is Christ. Let us adorn ourselves with the beautiful expression of Christ. Live a life worthy unto the Lord. Please him, be fruitful in every good work and increase in the knowledge of Christ. The key is Christ increasing in us. As he does, we will take off the old robe, the old man, our lower nature, and put on the new robe which is in Christ.

As the day of Christ's appearing approaches, may we be found as Esther, fully prepared to wear the crown. When her big day came, all her preparation paid off. The long year of bathing and all the other requirements had been completed. She was externally beautiful but also her internal beauty which was Christ was evident. She was clothed in all his virtues and the King was drawn to her scent! Her preparation was worth it and so is ours. I encourage you today to be clothed in Christ and Crowned with his glory.

The Cry of the Shulamite, "I will not Let Him Go"

Oh, the beautiful book of Song of Solomon. I must say what a song it is. It sings of melodies of love and music to the ears. This book is a love song that sings of Christ's love for Israel, his chosen people, his espoused bride. This particular book is written and arranged like scenes in a play. The imagery in the description of the words becomes so revealing and gives insight to the depth of love that is being expressed between the two. Their love and relationship are on a journey of coming to know one another and the goal is for the two to become one. From studying this book, I see that the Shulamite women did not know what all love would cost her. It was a journey that carried her into many different places and situations as she ran after her lover. Oh! But apparently it was worth it because once she found him, she said *"Now that I have found the one whom my soul loves I will not let him go."* (Song of Solomon 3:4) Usually we don't just stumble upon a desired treasure. In order to find something you have to search for it. Search requires journey. Jeremiah 29:13 tell us if we search for him wholeheartedly, we will find him just like the Shulamite found her lover.

I'm drawn back to my high school days of drama class. We discussed many plays and poems and did different role plays. One of the poems that we discussed was "How Do I Love Thee?" written by Elizabeth

Barrett in 1845. Her sonnet unveils her heart and the depth of emotion she felt for her lover. She had such an intensity of love that she said "How do I love thee? Let me count the ways." I'm sure you are familiar with the poem. In another expression of her love, she says "I love thee to the depth and breadth and height". Truly Elizabeth recognized that love grows and increases over time and through experience. She recognized that love has a depth, a breadth and height in a relationship, I totally concur based on the word of God as we can see in Ephesians 3:17-18 AMP

> [17]*so that Christ may dwell in your hearts through your faith. And may you, having been [deeply] rooted and [securely] grounded in love,* [18]*be fully capable of comprehending with all the saints (God's people) the width and length and height and depth of His love [fully experiencing that amazing, endless love]*

God's love is endless because he is endless and eternal. Through journeying we are able to experience the different levels of love as our relationship changes and grows. When I think of how much God loves me, I know because he gave his life for me. That is one supreme way he proved he loves me and you. Love covers all. *"No greater love than this than a man lay down his life for his friend."* (John 15:13.) Love can be explained to a certain degree but only true love is experienced. It is proven by the giving of ourselves to others. Christ desires we experience him as we grow in our relationship with him. He wants us to become close and intimate with him as we walk along our daily journeys. As cited in Genesis 5:5, Enoch walked with God and God took him. Enoch had become so close and intimate with God that he took him. When you walk closely with someone and come to know them you began to take on their mannerisms. The more you walk with them, the more trusting you become. You start to open the door of your heart and share yourself. This process allows you to become more vulnerable. Even though you may not fully give your trust, you become willing and allow yourself to take a risk. As you began to unveil yourself in the relationship this allows new levels of love to come forth, the depth, length, and the width. Consent for Christ to come close must be granted. In Song of Solomon 1:4-5 the Shulamite started out not having much confidence in herself. She didn't like how she looked because she toiled in the vineyards all day. But she said "Draw me and we will run." That was the consent the bridegroom needed. I encourage you to read the book if you haven't and find out how the story ends. Trust me it has a good ending. I will say it a thousand times - it's a journey of love as we are drawn out to Christ. It's necessary if we want to be joined to him in union.

I am thankful Christ took a risk when he went to the cross and died for you and me. He died knowing that not all would receive him. That's love and love is costly. Love cost Christ his earthly life, but look what he gained! Look what WE gained!

The love chapter I Corinthians 13 is the most revealing and unveiling picture of the love of God. Love is the sum total of who God is. This beautiful chapter gives us a perfect example of the many facets of love. Let take a peek at the AMP version.

> *⁴Love endures with patience and serenity,, love is kind and thoughtful,, and is not jealous or envious;; love does not brag and is not proud or arrogant.⁵It is not rude; it is not self-seeking, it is not provoked [nor overly sensitive and easily angered]; it does not take into account a wrong endured.⁶It does not rejoice at injustice, but rejoices with the truth [when right and truth prevail].⁷Love bears all things [regardless of what comes], believes all things [looking for the best in each one], hopes all things [remaining steadfast during difficult times], endures all things [without weakening].*

> *⁸Love never fails [it never fades nor ends]. But as for prophecies, they will pass away; as for tongues, they will cease; as for the gift of special knowledge, it will pass away.*

Oh, how I love this version; it is self-explanatory. It is God's love in us that will endure, be patient, kind, thoughtful, not jealous, not self-seeking and all the other things mentioned. So, in reference to our relationship with Christ, am I able to be patient with him when situations and circumstance in my life don't go as planned? Will I allow his love in me to cause me to bear up under all things as he is leading me to deeper paths unto a relationship with him? The Shulamite women had many highs and lows as she sought for her lover. She didn't realize how costly the relationship would be and all that it would cost her, as it will cost us. But oh! When we find him and experience him in the many different levels, the direction of our heart begins to be filled with greater love for him as he woos us and gives us an appetite for him. The Shulamite women was relentless in her pursuit. At the beginning of the chapter in verse 2 she had scent of his good ointment and finally came to the point where she realized "his banner over me is love." He who is the banner of love covered her as it does us. I believe that banner of love was a form of protection over her heart and a guard so that no other lover would steal her love.

Friends it all comes by way of journey. In this journey we will come to love him with our whole heart, mind, soul, spirit and all that is within us. Only when we walk day by day with God, as did Jesus and Enoch, will we come into a deeper and most personal intimate relationship. Christ is so in love with his Bride he is relentless and will fight for her. The Shulamite is representation of the church, the bride. Christ is calling us to a deeper and more intimate love. We cannot love someone we barely know. We must spend time with them, dine with them, grow a deep relationship.

I encourage us today if we have not entered a personal intimate relationship with Christ that this day will be the start of a new and deeper relationship. It starts by journey, giving Christ consent to draw you as he did the Shulamite women. He does the drawing. The scripture says, *"No man comes unless the spirit draws him."* (John 6:44) Once he draws you, I know you to will say as the Shulamite *"Now that I found the one whom my soul loves I will* not *let him go."* Let's pray.

Heavenly father, today we come humbly with our heart turned toward you. We ask that you would draw us unto you unto a deep personal relationship with you. Please come and scatter all outside lovers waiting to come in and seal my heart. We trust you this day and look to you in all things. Please forgive us where we have fallen short in our relationship with you. This day I desire to know you and am willing to risk it all for you because you are love and I need you. You are the perfect one that will make everything that concerns me right and good. I desire your will for my life. I surrender myself. Have your way in my life this day now and forever. I look forward to our new journey. In Jesus name I pray. Amen.

His Presence is Ever Present

There is nothing like being in the presence of someone you absolutely love, like, and adore. Especially when your spirits connect in thought, feeling and emotion. It's good to hang out with likeminded people. It's like there is a transference of their persons, meaning their joy, hope, expectation, laughter, love, and wisdom. When it's time for them to leave you hate to see them go and it seems the time passed too fast. You are left asking yourself, "Where did the time go?" And then you may notice that though they are physically absent, they left an impartation in you of what they had. If you were down in the dumps before they came, their presence has brightened your day. If you were troubled, their joy may have infected you and brought peace to you. I find that type of example in I Corinthians 16:17 NIV

I was glad when Stephanas, Fortunatus, and Achaicus arrived, because they have supplied what was lacking from you.

Reminds me of Mary and Martha. Mary sat at Jesus' feet and was blessed. The word says she received the good part. Christ is the good part because God is good. Martha however, though with good intentions, was busy preparing a meal for Jesus and was concerned that her sister was not helping. Mary was wise and steeped in her moment of visitation with the father. She presented herself at his feet as she set in his presence. Those times of visitations leave you looking forward to the next. You can't wait because you have been so blessed and filled with expectation of what the next visit will bring.

For me it's no different when I meet and fellowship with the Lord. His presence fills the room of my heart and no matter what type of day I am having, my spirit is lifted because of his presence. Everything has changed. My cloudy thoughts of worry and confusion lift like a fog. I no longer need to try to figure out how to handle situation because being in his presence brings clarity. My day and life become filled with new strength, hope, laughter and expectation of what's to come. I have become encouraged. When Jesus walks into the room of our hearts, situations change. His presence transforms everything because he is light and life. A good example would be the sun. If you sit out in it long enough you will become tan or even burned if not careful. A change has taken place; transference from the rays of the sun to your skin has transformed you.

I recall near the end of the year of 2022 I began to pray and seek the Lord in reference to the coming year for myself. I strive to seek his direction and will for my life as I am his and his life is mine. As I prayed and listened for him, he responded and said "The year 2023 will be a year of my presence. I will draw you closer to me in our relationship." I always pray "Lord draw me and I will come running because I can't draw myself." I am learning in this walk with Christ that being totally dependent on him is a beautiful thing. When I am weak only then am I made strong. I admit at times it gets frustrating and once again I return to his presence and wait for him to refresh me. I ask him to come and make me ready to be his bride and meet him. I must say I have not always been perfect in this journey with the Lord but Christ the perfect one has been perfecting me by his presence along the way.

The Bible says in Hebrew 12:6

> *For the LORD disciplines those he loves, and he punishes each one he accepts as his child."*

I understand being chastened by the Lord is uncomfortable and even painful, but being corrected by the Lord is necessary. I am glad because that means I am loved. God is not asking us to be perfect, but to have a perfect heart toward him. Chastening is not meant to

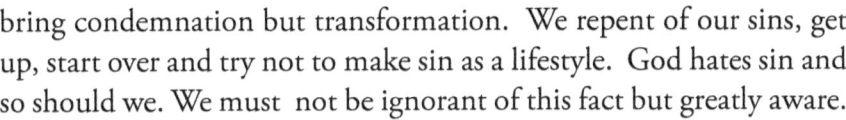

bring condemnation but transformation. We repent of our sins, get up, start over and try not to make sin as a lifestyle. God hates sin and so should we. We must not be ignorant of this fact but greatly aware.

Acts 18:38 declares

> [30] *"God overlooked people's ignorance about these things in earlier times, but now he commands everyone everywhere to repent of their sins and turn to him.*
>
> [31] *For he has set a day for judging the world with justice by the man he has appointed, and he proved to everyone who this is by raising him from the dead."*

Willful sinning is serious and we will severely be judged. Can you hear the sounding of the trumpet? Walking with God is serious business.

The Webster definition of presence is something (such as a spirit) felt or believed to be present. However, we want to look at the deeper spiritual meaning of the word. Looking at the Greek meaning often brings a clearer understanding. The Greek word for presence is Parousia which means personal presence and also can be related to the second coming of Christ. Another meaning is a visit by a person or their personal presence. How many know when you accepted Christ, he entered your Spirit? It is the entering of Christ in our spirit that changes us and make us ready to meet Christ. The word says *"Christ in us is the hope of glory."* (Colossians 1:27) Christ in us is his presence. To the degree we obey and submit to his will to the degree his presence. The more we submit to Christ, the more our relationship will increase and become greater and greater. Just as we have five natural senses, taste, touch, see, hear, smell see, we also have those same senses in our spirit where Christ dwells. If you notice, right in the center of the word heart, where Christ lives, you find the word ear. You will hear his voice in your ear. But of course, first you must learn to recognize his voice. That comes by spending time with him. Have you ever said or heard someone say 'I sense this or that?' That is the spiritual senses. Those spiritual senses are fine-tuned by relationship.

Our lives must become living sacrifices for Christ and that comes by way of the cross. *"Not I live but Christ lives in me."* (Galations 2:20) As our relationship begins to grow as we walk with Christ, he becomes closer and closer and we began to hear his voice clearer and clear. The more we hear his voice, the more his presence in our lives begins to increase. David recognized the importance of having the presence of God near when he said in Psalms 51:11 NLT

> *"Do not banish me from your presence, and don't take your Holy Spirit from me."*

David knew the presence of God was everything and all that he needed was found in the presence of God. The life of Enoch is a perfect example as he walked close to and with God, God took him. Enoch has become so close to God that apparently Christ wanted him to be with him. In these dark days all that we need will be found in the presence of God. When God visits us his people and when we submit to his leading, we sense him in everything we do. When God comes close nothing in our lives will remain the same. The scripture says, *"In his presence is fullness of joy."* (Psalms 16:11) *"Thou wilt shew me the path of life: in thy presenceisfullness of joy; at thy right handthere arepleasures for evermore."*

I can say, the presence of the Holy Spirit is everything to me and for me. He is the main ingredient. It's kind of like baking a homemade cake. Even if you have followed every instruction but forgot one little thing, it won't be perfect. If you forget to add the baking soda or baking powder there will be no rising of the cake. It's no different in our lives. Without the rising of the Holy Spirit in our lives, our lives will be spiritually flat. We need the most critical ingredient, the presence of his Holy Spirit, to arise to the potential God has set for us. Once God arises, his enemies are scattered. The word says let God arise. He will not arise in our lives if he is not the main ingredient. So, I too say strongly as David, *"Lord, take not thy presence from me."* (Psalm 51:11) Let that be the cry of our hearts today. My life is ordered by this one fact: his presence means and is everything to me. Let God arise on the inside.

Don't know about you, but when I look around at the world I live in, it is dark. It's hard to find joy with so much crime, murder, lies, and deception apart from Christ. Oh! But when I get in the presence of the Lord, when the Lord comes in visitation and makes his presence known in my day to day life, everything changes We must journey with God and allow him to make us ready to meet him as things are changing quickly.

Matthew 24:37-39 NLT

37 "When the Son of Man returns, it will be like it was in Noah's day.

38 In those days before the flood, the people were enjoying banquets and parties and weddings right up to the time Noah entered his boat.

39 People didn't realize what was going to happen until the flood came and swept them all away. That is the way it will be when the Son of Man comes.

I used to believe I always have tomorrow. But no man knows the day nor the hour the son of man will return. (Matthew 24:6) His return will be sudden and surprising. If not careful, it will catch some of God's people off guard. We are living in the age of selfie. Self-love, self-gratifications, self-centeredness. This type of self-preoccupation will catch the world unaware. Lord, help us to awaken and see the signs of the time and realize how much you love us. We need the Lord to help us realize he is drawing us unto himself, not things, position, or people. For it's in his presence we are made whole.

My heart's cry and passion in today's journal is that we his people *and* the lost be awakened to God. Awaken to his every abiding presence in us which makes him close to us. I have always heard and believed we each have as much or as little of God as we want. It's a sacrifice that we must make for his ever-growing and increasing presence in our lives. We must have a sense of uninterrupted readiness and anticipation. We must be constantly growing and increasing in Christ. This is the journey I have been on. Join me! May your lives be richly blessed with an unprecedented love and hunger for Christ now and in the days ahead. My prayer for you today is that you will open your heart in a greater way so that the presence of Christ will walk in your room and you will never be the same.

> *⁷Dear brothers and sisters,[a] be patient as you wait for the Lord's return. Consider the farmers who patiently wait for the rains in the fall and in the spring. They eagerly look for the valuable harvest to ripen.⁸ You, too, must be patient. Take courage, for the coming of the Lord is near.* James 5:7

Maranatha, Our Lord Come!

Choosing of a Bride
part 1 "Vashti"

The choosing of a bride from the spiritual perspective is all about divine distinction. God is a God of distinction. Christ is very deliberate and methodical in choosing his bride. The Lord instructed Israel, his people, not to marry foreign wives but we see in I Kings his word was not heeded.

I Kings 11:1 NLT

Now King Solomon loved many foreign women. Besides Pharaoh's daughter, he married women from Moab, Ammon, Edom, Sidon, and from among the Hittites. ²The Lord had clearly instructed the people of Israel, "You must not marry them, because they will turn your hearts to their gods." Yet Solomon insisted on loving them anyway. ³He had 700 wives of royal birth and 300 concubines. And in fact, they did turn his heart away from the Lord.

⁴In Solomon's old age, they turned his heart to worship other gods instead of being completely faithful to the Lord his God, as his father, David, had been. ⁵Solomon worshiped Ashtoreth, the goddess of the Sidonians, and Molech, [a] the detestable god of the Ammonites. ⁶In this way, Solomon did what was evil in the Lord's sight; he refused to follow the Lord completely, as his father, David, had done.

God is about wholeheartedness toward him. He will not accept a part-time lover. A mixture is a compromise rooted in a divided heart and unacceptable to God. Solomon refused to follow the Lord COMPLETELY. God is an all or nothing God and will not accept anything less. He will not accept a little bit of me and a little bit of him all mixed up and call it a relationship. Neither will he accept a little of my way and a little of his way. He will have no rivals. We can see from Solomon when the word says he didn't follow me fully. Sin is evil in the eyes of God and we should view it as such.

Vashi and Esther are both representations of a type of bride and also representation of a church type, as we are the church and not merely the place we attend. The Hebrew word for distinction is pala, which means to set apart and deal with differently. The Webster dictionary explains the word distinction as the act of separating or distinguishing, a mark of difference. There is and always will be a clear difference between those who are Christ's and those who are not. Paul said in II Corinthians to *"Come out from amongst them and be separate, touch not the unclean things."* Another reference to separation is found in

I Peter 2:9 ESV

> *"But you are a chosen race, a royal priesthood, a holy nation, a people for his own possession that you may proclaim the excellencies of him who called you out of darkness into his marvelous light."*

We belong to Christ and are his possession. There is a clear distinction from those who are his and those who are not. His people are royal, holy and possessed by him and him alone. God's people are divinely distinct, peculiar. Peculiar means God's own possession. God's very own people are an obedient people. Christ has total possession of his bride. If not, what else are we allowing to possess us? Of course, this possession is an inside journey. Christ in us does a work if we allow him. This work comes by way of an increase of Christ. His life in us will increase and our own life will decrease. Jesus on the inside and working on the outside!

The brides Christ chooses are distinct in their consecration and love for their God, distinct in their passion for God. Above all, their love for God and undivided heart for God are what sets them apart. Everything with God has always been about distinction and separation when it comes down to those that are his. Distinctions are clearly seen between day and night, the sun and the moon, the wheat from the tare. I love how the Lord is so meticulous even in nature. Each animal has a distinct sound and is known. Some fly, some crawl, some hop. But one thing about it, you cannot mix up a frog with a grasshopper. Though they both jump they are distinct in looks and nature. God is awesome and wise and I love him. The Lord has never been about mixture in anything and his distinction is very defining.

We each will choose the type of bride we want to be or become along our journey. As he chooses us, may we choose him. Christ has given us a great example in his word of the type of bride he will be joined to and not be joined to. This journal will be two parts as we will look at two brides, Vashti and Esther. Both Vashti and Esther were beautiful women. The distinction between the two is clear; Vashti had only external beauty but Esther had both internal and external. Esther had a heart that loved God. The story of Vashti is a sad story. She started out great but somewhere along her journey her love grew cold for her lover, her king Ahasuerus.

Unfortunately, it runs parallel to the churches of Ephesus and Laodicea in Revelation. One left their first love and sadly the other grew lukewarm. Queen Vashti was wife of King Ahasuerus. She was the Queen of Persia and Media. I thought it was interesting when I began to research and found sited in the Ultimate Bible Dictionary her name Vashti means 'the once desired, the beloved.' WOW! Once desired - she lived out the meaning of her name. The toppling of her reign came when she refused the King, her husband's request to come and show her beauty as he entertained in the palace Shushan. In those days, to approach the King even though being married to him he had to extend the scepter. Even the Queen could not approach him unless the scepter was extended. The only exception was if the King actually summoned the Queen. Then she could just enter his presence. On that day no scepter was necessary as he called for her. However, on the same day Vashti made a feast for the women in the royal house which belonged to King Ahasuerus (Esther 1:9-19). Vashti chose not to come before the King and rejected the King's command. She stayed with the women and did not go before the King. Of course, that angered the King. The King was very wroth and his anger burned in him. It wasn't long before Vashti was punished. She had disobeyed the laws in the land that states *all* must follow the commandments of the King. She not only had done wrong to the King but also to all the princes and to all the people that are in the provinces of the King. (Esther 1:16) Because Vashti chose not to obey, her crown was taken, she was banished from the palace and another was to be chosen to take her place.

My goodness what a horrendous ending to a once beautiful life and marriage. It all came down to a choice of who she loved and what she loved. Obviously, she loved herself more. She had the things and life of a queen. She had all the benefits but didn't want the King. It's kind of what I have noticed in some people; they want the things of God but not the God of all things. They are comfortable with having his name and all benefits that come with that name, but refuse to be totally possessed and committed to him. Ahhh! But just as King Ahasuerus wouldn't have it, neither will God. He is an all or nothing God. There is only one true bride. That is one who loves Christ with her whole, heart, mind soul and strength. The Lord should capture the heart of his bride in such a way that it causes us to allow him to gain complete commitment of our life and becomes everything to us. I will say it a hundred times my friends, it's a journey unto becoming. I am journeying unto this kind of relationship and find the more I yield, he gains a greater possession of my heart. He draws me unto him and I am coming to know him. To be honest, we will not and cannot trust anyone fully unless we know him. Trust is gained by growth in relationship. Let us be encouraged to know that when we call for Christ he will come. He is faithful.

As I said at the beginning Vashti and Esther are representation of a bride/church spiritually. We can learn from both Brides. As I have said before and will say again, it is important that we each study to show ourselves approved unto God. You must research and study. Just don't take my word because the word says it Proverbs 25:2,

"It isthe glory of God to conceal a matter. But the glory of kingsisto search out a matter" Search it out and let the Lord himself reveal to you what the Spirit is saying to the church. The Lord never will give only one person all revelation because the word is of no private interpenetrations.

Vashti obviously left her first love as did the church in Revelation. She walked off and left her first love. She became independent of her husband and no longer desired to be submitted unto him. She went her own way leaning to her own understanding. The self-willed independent Spirit, my friend, will destroy us. In my earlier walk with the Lord as he was dealing with my heart and commitment unto him, he said "Rochelle, to be selfish is to self-destruct." WOW! That was a shock and awe moment for me as I had to make some decisions in my walk with him. I had to relinquish some things that were not his will for my life, though it was painful and I did not understand all the reasoning. It was not clear. As time went on, I now can see why. Nonetheless I said yes Lord and he has been with me helping me along this challenging journey. God is good, faithful, loving and patient. Know that he cares much for you today. Be encouraged, my brothers and sisters. Marriage is about union with Christ, becoming one. We lay down our lives that Christ may live. I see such a resemblance in the church. Not being critical but what I see and the Lord has personally revealed to me is that there is a lot of self-centeredness in the church. *My* gift, *my* calling, *my* this and that. I'm hearing very little of Christ as life. I have found Christ is a packaged deal. Christ said he came to do the will of his father. I never read once where he petitions his father for anything of selfish value or gain. Let me know, I could be wrong. I am not sure if Vashti thought she was immune from consequences. She wanted to have her cake and eat it to. God is no respecter of persons and his word will always remain the same. There will always be consequences for our sins regardless of how long it takes for the consequences to hit our door.

I understand from the example of Vashti what happens if I choose to walk away from my first love. I have taken this example and compared it to my own life as a caution to my walk with God. I am able to make adjustments in my journey of preparation so I do not end up as Vashti, She was a Bride that was kicked out just as Adam and Eve were banished from the garden because of sin. My hope today is that we realize how crucial are these times we are living in. The days are evil and dark. Without knowing this God, we are helpless. You know the Bible tell us in II Peter 3:12, *"Looking forward to the day of God and hurrying it along. On that day, he will set the heavens on fire, and the elements will melt away in the flames."*

We can hasten the coming of the Lord by making ourselves ready to meet him, and allowing him to make us ready. Don't know about you, but I am looking forward to his return as this planet has become so evil. I too am like Lot in 11 Peter 2:7. God rescued Lot out of Sodom because he was a righteous man who was sick of the shameful immorality of the wicked people around him. I am vexed at the evil and lawlessness, how about you? May we make ourselves ready to meet our groom. Come into right relationship so that we may be joined to him.

In closing may we choose not to be a bride in representation to Vashti. May we become so totally possessed by Christ and his love for us that things will never take his place in our hearts. May we choose to never be a bride that will leave her first love and be banished from his presence. Maranatha!

Choosing of a Bride
part 2 "Esther"

When I think about Esther, I am drawn to Proverbs 31:29 AMP.

"Many daughters have done nobly, and well [with the strength of character that is steadfast in goodness], But you excel them all."

My goodness what an example to follow. What a standing ovation to one who excels them all. Esther was a woman of noble character. Esther and Ruth are the only two women who have books in the Bible. That alone to me speaks volumes and is very noteworthy. It was once said by a man of God "How we live is a window of our heart others peer though" It could not have been said better. All throughout the word of God as we read, we are peering through the lives of those that have gone on before us. Their individual journeys, some noble and some not so noble, stand as instruction for us. In the book of Proverbs, we find the nature of the living Christ toward his Bride. As I have previously stated, the church is an archetype of the bride. Peering through the book of Proverbs we see Christ, his bride in noble character and the living expression of the bride. She speaks fitly spoken words of wisdom, virtuous, a helper and strengthener. Because the word says the two shall become one you cannot separate Christ from his bride in expression of life. As I have previous mentioned, Esther was an orphan raised by her cousin. At that time Esther lived under the reign of the Persian King Ahasuerus. Esther was a beautiful

Jewish orphan girl. Her beauty was not only in her appearance but a light in her heart. The light of the spirit of God and her love for him shone in her everyday life.

In Esther's day there was much conflict in the reign of King Ahasuerus and a hidden plot to destroy all the Jews. Esther's Jewish name is Hadassah. How many know there is a specific time for an arising and coming out in our lives? Not only in our lives, but to come out to God. Being born for such a time as this was Esther's arising in time of conflict in Persia. God always has divine providence, meaning a way by which he directs all things toward a purpose. At the time of Esther's arising, Babylonia was in captivity and God's divine providence was at work. God will always arise and fight for his bride! He has a set time for the one he loves, and it is not man's time ever.

The beauty of this story for me is first the love and commitment she had for her God. Her love was the foundation of this story and why today we are reading about it in the word of God. God is love, period! Love covers and conquers a multitude of sin; love is not selfish and looks on the things of another. Esther's love for God is what gave her courage to stand alone and being willing to risk her life. Let us realize love is costly and rewarding at the same time. Remember, all brides stand alone. There is only one bride at the altar. At the altar of our lives, it's us and God who have chosen to become one. I can tell you getting to that point is a journey. Many times, people will start out with others who say they want to go all the way with God but as time goes on they drop off because the price was too great. In the book of Esther, many maidens were gathered together in Shushan the palace to the custody of Hegai, the keeper of the women. It reminds me of the scripture Matthew 22:14 *"Many are called but few are chosen."* There is journey between being called and being chosen. Our way of life will decide for us, meaning our decisions and actions. We will be required to yield to Christ and his way alone.

I Corinthians 10:23 says

All things are lawful [that is, morally legitimate, permissible], but not all things are beneficial or advantageous. All things are lawful, but not all things are constructive [to character]and edifying [to spiritual life]." This is where our choices and decisions come. They will affect how we progress in our journey of readiness and becoming one with the Lord.

What I love about Christ's bride is her divine distinction. He always makes sure his people are a distinct people which signifies they are his. Esther was set-apart, distinct. She found favor. She didn't have to push her way through to be seen, noticed, chosen, or favored because God's divine providence was at work and the Spirit of Christ was within her. I love it. Christ will provide his bride with everything she needs to be dressed and ready to meet him. In Esther 2:13 the AMP because she found favor with Hegai, the king provided Esther with everything she needed for purification and he even gave her seven maidens to help her in her preparation.

Christ gives us the Holy Spirit our Helper to help us prepare to meet him. Christ will make us ready as long as our love for him is our foundation, as it was for Esther.

When reading and studying about Esther's life I can see that her journey entails process. Step by step the Lord led her. She was first gathered up with all the other virgins, a process in her journey. Then she was chosen among many other maidens, a process in her journey. She entered in the king's palace, a process in her journey. Finally, she became queen. Can you see the journey unto preparation? Esther could not have missed any steps along her journey; each step of her journey led to the next. You know, our lives are no different. We are each on a journey. If we are not on the journey Christ has laid for us, we are still on some type of journey. Guess what? All journeys lead to a destination be it the one we desire or the one that we fall into. I'm sure we can all attest to what happens when our navigation system has a mind of its own and gives us the wrong directions or takes us miles out of the way when it could have been avoided. Let us live on purpose and awaken and arise.

Esther's time of arising was pivotal in her time for a people and nation. The Jews were set to be destroyed by a wicked plot of Haman. But God!

Esther 4:8-15 NLT

⁸Mordecai gave Hathach a copy of the decree issued in Susa that called for the death of all Jews. He asked Hathach to show it to Esther and explain the situation to her. He also asked Hathach to direct her to go to the king to beg for mercy and plead for her people.⁹So Hathach returned to Esther with Mordecai's message.

¹⁰Then Esther told Hathach to go back and relay this message to Mordecai:¹¹"All the king's officials and even the people in the provinces know that anyone who appears before the king in his inner court without being invited is doomed to die unless the king holds out his gold scepter. And the king has not called for me to come to him for thirty days."¹²So Hathach[a]gave Esther's message to Mordecai.

¹³Mordecai sent this reply to Esther: "Don't think for a moment that because you're in the palace you will escape when all other Jews are killed.¹⁴If you keep quiet at a time like this, deliverance and relief for the Jews will arise from some other place, but you and your relatives will die. Who knows if perhaps you were made queen for just such a time as this?"

¹⁵Then Esther sent this reply to Mordecai:¹⁶"Go and gather together all the Jews of Susa and fast for me. Do not eat or drink for three days, night or day. My maids and I will do the same. And then, though it is against the law, I will go in to see the king. If I must die, I must die."¹⁷So Mordecai went away and did everything as Esther had ordered him.

For this moment Esther was born. I love the line that says 'for such a time as this.' Every part of her journey led her to this pivotal moment. The moment of arising or choosing to die, if necessary, in order to save a people. The word says *"To die is to gain, to save your life is to lose it."* (Philippians 1:21). Love is all about laying our lives down and as I've said before we must risk it all on Christ, even if it's difficult, even if we are alone. Esther's journey along the way had prepared her. She was a woman of prayer, consecration, and distinction. Her heart belonged to the Lord. Her journey taught her wisdom because she was connected to the one who *is* wisdom. Her kindness helped others and it was God's gentleness that made her great in the journey. Such a bold and fearless women who trusted in her God! We cannot trust anyone we do not know. This journey is about coming to know Christ. Each journey has a mission in our lives and it should be that the Christ within is growing and increasing in us as we allow him to. He must have his way.

The Esther bride is one of strength, honor, courage, yielded, lovely, gentle, kind, meek, fearless, bold, a lover of God and people. The Esther bride is a warrior! Warriors don't just die, they die fighting if necessary. Process leads to preparation for the bride. We are in a time of both, process and preparation. The church is the bride of Christ. But the one that makes herself ready is the true bride. As in Esther's day there were many virgins, but only one bride.

I find many similarities of Esther's day and ours. You may ask how? Well, Esther was a Jew and Satan had a hit man named Haman. He had his plans to destroy God's people. We can see this in our day as well. Christ's people are being silenced and free speech is slowly taken away. Our children are being taken from us by the government which should be for the people. We have the spirit of homosexuality rising as though God created it. We have a land that's being invaded and a church that for the most part is asleep and lazy. Excuse me in advance if I step on some toes. You will find more church goers at a little league game, football games, fall festivals and everything else before you find them at a weekly prayer meeting. Most only go to church on a Sunday and through the week they never open their Bible or pray. Children are allowed to be on social media for hours but never given a Bible study lesson. We wonder why we have a hit man Satan that has gained so much ground in this nation. It saddens my heart.

When the hit man Satan by way of Haman embarked upon Esther's territory he got quite a surprise. What was the first word Esther sent back to Mordecai? Call for a time of fasting and prayer. Have a solemn assembly. PRAY. How many know prayer is a weapon of war? Prayer first humbles us; it causes us to have hearts of contrition and repentance. We can see by the ending of the story what happened. Prayer allowed God to get involved, the humbling of a people and nation allowed God to take control. It is and will be no different for us. It's time we wake up, my brothers and sisters. It's time we humble ourselves, repent, forsake our evil ways and turn back to God. Put him in the right place of our lives. We are meant to be a warrior bride. It is through you and me that Christ will arise and work. Through an Esther Bride, God will be allowed to do his eternal will. Will we let him? Oh Esther, your day of arising has come! Is there not a cause to fight?

The Warrior Bride

Reflect back to the statement Mordecai made in the book of Esther in verse 4:13-14.

> *¹³Mordecai sent this reply to Esther: "Don't think for a moment that because you're in the palace you will escape when all other Jews are killed.¹⁴If you keep quiet at a time like this, deliverance and relief for the Jews will arise from some other place, but you and your relatives will die. Who knows if perhaps you were made queen for just such a time as this?"*

So I ask us today, is there not a cause to fight? Surely you do not believe if we do nothing at all everything will still be well. Do you think it will still be okay even if if we choose not to fight? We can never appease, pacify, or placate our enemy the Devil, Satan. We must come to realize that, just as God has an eternal plan and purpose for his people, so does Satan. Evil Haman in the book of Esther was being used by Satan to destroy God's people; it's no different for us today. John 10:10 alerts us to the fact the enemy comes only to kill, steal, and destroy; that's his mission. Sadly, I must admit he's doing a bang-up job in this nation as well as in the church. There has not been much resistance against him as he has come for our relationship with Christ, our health, our families, our schools and nation, and so much more. I say that because Christ said *"Ye are the light of the world,"* (Matthew 5:14) But yet, our nation is so dark. Why? Our light is dim and fading fast.

One of Satan's best tactics is to come in and try to steal the Christ within us. You may ask how does he do that? In the book of Mark, it speaks of the parable of the sower. For times sake I encourage you to read the whole parable for scriptural context as I will only be focusing on one point. The parable is very self-explanatory which is beautiful. That's why the Lord used parables - so anyone could understand them. Mark 4:15 lets us know these are they by the way side, where the word is sown; but when they have heard, Satan cometh immediately, and taketh away the word that was sown in their hearts. Christ is the living word hid in our heart and is our foundation. If Satan is successful to over-crowd our hearts with the cares of this world his strategy will be successful.

As we look all around us and over our nation and the nations of the earth we see killing, destruction, defilement and many other evils I could name. I'd say Satan is on his job carrying out his mission. However, my question for us today is, have we the church, God's people become so comfortable and tolerant to the evil that is has desensitized us or brought us to the spirit of disillusionment? The good news is the Lord is a Warrior. Exodus 15:3 reads, *"The Lord is warrior, The Lord is his name."* The definition of warrior in the dictionary is one who is engaged or experienced in battle, a soldier. Did you catch it? A soldier is a man engaged in warfare. From this we can see and agree warriors are in a fight. Jesus said it himself, *"I came to destroy the works of the Devil."* (I John 3:8). Christ is now seated at the right hand of the father and has given authority in his name to cast out Devils.

(Mark 3:16)

He has made the enemy our footstool but we must still fight and secure the victory on a person level in our lives.

Jeremiah 20:11 in the NLT reads

But the LORD stands beside me like a great warrior. Before him my persecutors will stumble. They cannot defeat me. They will fail and be thoroughly humiliated. Their dishonor will never be forgotten.

That is a word to shout on! The Lord is with us! All throughout the Old Testament they were always at war, conquering, overthrowing. Sometimes they themselves were conquered but always fighting and engaged in the fight. The Lord tells us the battle is already won but we still must go down to the battle field and fight. We still must engage in the battle. This engagement in battle allows us to become experienced warriors. God trains our hands to war (Psalms 144:1). David became a great warrior and Goliath was not a threat to him. He had already killed a lion and bear while being a shepherd boy attending his father's sheep. Let us take a glance at his training in I Samuel 17:34-37 NLT

> *34But David said to Saul, "Your servant has been keeping his father's sheep. When a lion or a bear came and carried off a sheep from the flock,35I went after it, struck it and rescued the sheep from its mouth. When it turned on me, I seized it by its hair, struck it and killed it.36Your servant has killed both the lion and the bear; this uncircumcised Philistine will be like one of them, because he has defied the armies of the living God.37TheLordwho rescued me from the paw of the lion and the paw of the bear will rescue me from the hand of this Philistine. "Saul said to David, "Go, and the Lord be with you. "*

My God! First look at the Lord our warrior through David's fight with the Giant. Now let's see David's progression in war. He first killed a bear and pulled the sheep from its mouth. His hand was being trained to war. A little shepherd boy guarding the sheep, no doubt probably a little fearful but he was engaged in battle being trained. Who knew that one day he would kill the big giant Goliath? When everyone was fearful and no candidates were found to take down the giant, the little shepherd boy stepped up. The one who had been trained for war slew the giant. This lesson teaches us that at some point we must be engaged in the fight. But first we must be trained to be a warrior. We must be prepared. It's been said victory is SWEET! It sure is. Victory is sweet because you now have a testimony of what God can do in and through you. Victory allows you to gain confidence while being engaged in any battle regardless of how big or how small the enemy seems to be. The mantra becomes "If God did it before he will do it again." I love it!

You may compare yourself to David in reference to the giant standing before. You may feel like the giant is so much bigger than you. It could be a giant of sickness and disease. A runaway child, a bad marriage. You may feel powerless, but I say, "Don't look at the giant but at the warrior Christ in you." Prepare for battle!

As David progressed in his life he is deemed as a man of war and he gathered a group of mighty men to fight with and for him. They were called David's Mighty men. I mean, these men were brutal and fierce. Nothing like being trained by the best! As always for the sake of time I will only mention part of the chapter for a point of reference. The history of the warriors and their feats of battle is amazing and encouraging (11 Samuel 23: 16-20). My thought has always been, "Warriors don't just die, they die fighting." I said it before and I repeat it now because I believe it so strongly. The scriptures prove it! When looking at some of these mighty men in battle, we can see how the Lord was with them and won great victories. In verse 10, one warrior fought till his hand stuck to his sword and the Lord wrought a great victory. In verse 12 another man slew the Philistines and the Lord wrought a great victory. In verse 16 three mighty men broke through the host of the Philistines and drew water out of the well of Bethlehem for their captain David. These mighty men were warriors in every sense of the word. If you noticed, though they were physically engaged in the battle, yet it says "AND THE LORD WROUGHT A GREAT VICTORY!" See it is the Lord who is our warrior. Isaiah 42:13 in the NIV is quoted, "*The Lord will march out like a champion, like a warrior he will stir up his zeal; with a shout he will raise the battle cry and will triumph over his enemies.*" WOW! With a shout! Oh! I'm sure you know about the shout in the story of Jericho. (Joshua 6:1-27) You can read it for yourself. The gist of the story once again is they had to go down to the battlefield to fight but it was the Lord that wrought a great victory. All they had to do was follow the instructions of the

Lord. As commanded, on the seventh day they shouted and the wall came down. That's the Lord our warrior.

I hope the history of the warriors that have gone on before us has inspired and awakened you to the fight. Engagement is necessary. I am sure some are wondering "What do we need to be fighting for as a warrior bride?" I say there is *so* much to be fought for! In the Lord's prayer it says *"Thy kingdom come thy will be done on earth as it is in heaven."* (Matthew 6:10) God has an eternal plan for man. He left us his power and authority. By way of prayer, we bring what is in heaven down to earth. Christ will fight to have his inheritance in his saints. We too must fight for that. He wants a bride that he has totally possessed for himself. We must fight for the church as Christ intends it to be, under the total rule and lordship of Christ and not man. We must fight that Christ return to his church. Most of church is like an assembly line. We sing two songs, we read the scripture, we take up offering and go through the motions. There isn't space on the program for the Spirit of Christ to move and have his way. We are the church and to the degree that the life of Christ is growing and increasing in us will be the degree the revealing of Christ will be in our services. We are fighting for Christ to have a people of his kind in life and nature. Christ in us is Christ through us; what's in comes out. We are fighting for God's rights over this earth and planet. We are fighting for our families. We are fighting that the government of Christ will be embraced in his church. We are the church. Christ must govern our lives and not we ourselves. I know it's a fight! I agree with Paul when he says, *"I try to do good yet evil is always present."* (Roman 7:15) The key to it all is, we become a bride filled with Christ, filled with his ruling presence and dominion that he may rule through us in this earthly realm. The stories we looked at showed us that Christ wrought the victory. It is no less for us. But we must prepare; we must become yielded vessels, his hands and feet on the earth. Simply put, we must spend time with God to be empowered and strengthened for the fight. We must be filled with his presence before we enter into any battle. There will be no victory without the presence of his Spirit within us.

Mighty warriors are those mighty in prayer. Their lives are committed and obedient to Christ. James 5:16 says *"The effectual fervent prayer of the righteous avails much."* Fervent prayer avails much. Prayer changes things, pulls down darkness, thwarts the enemy and so much more. When I started out on this journey over 12 years ago this was one of the first mandates and scripture the Lord gave me. He instructed me that I must become a woman of prayer. I can tell you starting out it was not easy rising early before dawn, before work. And sometimes I stayed up late into the night. This became a part of my training and has impacted my life greatly. Much has changed because of prayer. Health battles have been won, family battles have been won and so much more. I am grateful. Results did not come over night but I stayed on the battlefield engaged in war and just as he did for David's mighty men, he did it for me THE LORD WROUGHT THE VICTORY and he will do it for you if you are willing.

Let us be clear about something and look at Ephesians 6:10-18 NLT

> *[10]A final word: Be strong in the Lord and in his mighty power.[11]Put on all of God's armor so that you will be able to stand firm against all strategies of the devil.[12]For we[d] are not fighting against flesh-and-blood enemies, but against evil rulers and authorities of the unseen world, against mighty powers in this dark world, and against evil spirits in the heavenly places.*
>
> *[13]Therefore, put on every piece of God's armor so you will be able to resist the enemy in the time of evil. Then after the battle you will still be standing firm.[14]Stand your ground, putting on the belt of truth and the body armor of God's righteousness.[15]For shoes, put on the peace that comes from the Good News so that you will be fully prepared.[e][16]In addition to all of these, hold up the shield of faith to stop the fiery arrows of the devil.[f][17]Put on salvation as your helmet, and take the sword of the Spirit, which is the word of God.*
>
> *[18]Pray in the Spirit at all times and on every occasion. Stay alert and be persistent in your prayers for all believers everywhere.[g]*

We can clearly see we are in a battle and our enemy is an unseen one. One of the main strategies of the enemy is to get our focus only on what we see because he works unseen and covertly. It's so easy to take things at face value and accept the fact that things are just that away. NO! There are evil forces working against us. We see it in the scripture so we must be aware, engaged and fight. We must not let the Devil roam illegally in our lives and the lives our families without a confrontation and fight.

Let's look at Daniel and how his perseverance and consistency in prayer brought him results. He withstood the evil forces that were arrayed against him though he did not know his answer was being held up in prayer for 21 days. (Daniel 10:12-14)

> *[12] Then he said, "Don't be afraid, Daniel. Since the first day you began to pray for understanding and to humble yourself before your God, your request has been heard in heaven. I have come in answer to your prayer.[13] But for twenty-one days the spirit prince[c] of the kingdom of Persia blocked my way. Then Michael, one of the archangels,[d] came to help me, and I left him there with the spirit prince of the kingdom of Persia.[e] [14] Now I am here to explain what will happen to your people in the future, for this vision concerns a time yet to come."*

We can clearly see from this passage of scripture that yes God does hear and answer our prayer. As the old church saints use to say "He may not come when you want him but he's right on time." Amen. We simply must grasp the reality that prayer is war and battle and we must stay in the fight and know that God is working all things out for our good. (Romans 8:28) We must endure, persevere, and keep our eyes on God in expectancy. We are called to be soldiers enlisted in God's army. Now fight!

I would be remiss not mention the hall of fame of faith warriors in Hebrews 11 NLT. They had amazing feats of triumphant victories, and too some defeats. However the defeats were permitted for our good as we will see below. Hebrews 11:32-39

³²How much more do I need to say? It would take too long to recount the stories of the faith of Gideon, Barak, Samson, Jephthah, David, Samuel, and all the prophets.³³By faith these people overthrew kingdoms, ruled with justice, and received what God had promised them. They shut the mouths of lions,³⁴quenched the flames of fire, and escaped death by the edge of the sword. Their weakness was turned to strength. They became strong in battle and put whole armies to flight.³⁵Women received their loved ones back again from death.

But others were tortured, refusing to turn from God in order to be set free. They placed their hope in a better life after the resurrection.³⁶Some were jeered at, and their backs were cut open with whips. Others were chained in prisons.³⁷Some died by stoning, some were sawed in half,[d] and others were killed with the sword. Some went about wearing skins of sheep and goats, destitute and oppressed and mistreated.³⁸They were too good for this world, wandering over deserts and mountains, hiding in caves and holes in the ground.

³⁹All these people earned a good reputation because of their faith, yet none of them received all that God had promised.⁴⁰For God had something better in mind for us, so that they would not reach perfection without us.

These warriors fought believing God for the promise by faith and in faith. However, none of them received all that God had promised but died with a good reputation. That's amazing! They trusted and believed God all the way to the end. They are the example for us in our walk. Never to give up; preserver in the fight. They were unselfish warriors fighting, and one day we will reach perfection together.

May we awaken to war, fighting in faith, looking unto Jesus the author and finisher of our faith. The word of God exhorts us to walk circumspect, watching and praying. Habakkuk 2:1 9 illustrates how the prophet Habakkuk watched. He had a watchtower. He stood in the presence of God to hear what the Lord would say to him in prayer. As a watchman he had to be able to hear God. When you watch in prayer, you stand in the presence of God in a regular disciplined prayer life.

Consistency is the key. The consistency is what allows one to be able to hear the voice of God clearer and clearer. We each much personally come into the presence of God to watch and pray. As I have said many times in this journal you must study the word of God for yourself and gain greater dept of what the Lord is saying to you beyond what I am writing. He is our personal Lord and Savior. The Lord has allowed me to pen certain topics in this book in hopes to bring awareness to truth and get people to think about what they are thinking. Also, to pen topics that some people may have never heard that are relevant for our times and necessary for preparation in the days ahead. Remember a thief can only steal from the one that is unaware that he is lurking and operating covertly. Selah!

So today right now at this very moment, are you ready to fight, mighty warrior? We have much to fight for and much ground to cover. The fight begins right in our own homes, marriages, children, and the family of God. We fight for the blood right of the Lamb who died for his bride. We must say "Devil you will not have my children, my home, my family, and the house of God." They have been bought and paid for by the blood of the Lamb. We fight, stand and contended for the faith of God once delivered to us. Today let us come to the conclusion we will not back down, retreat, or be bullied by the kingdom of darkness. The blood right of the lamb trumps Satan and all of his power. What do you say? Let's fight warriors. So as the Lord said to Gideon in Judges 6:12 so I say to you *"The Lord is with you, O Valiant warrior"*.

I encourage the bride today, if you have not developed a personal relationship with the Lord, let today be the day. If you are one sitting on the sideline of the battle field, get in the fight. Our nations are near destruction. It's dark and we are the ones that Christ will arise in Isaiah 60. The trumpet is sounding loudly today. I know this journal has been long but the trumpet must be sounded. God is counting on you and me to co-labor with him and bring his kingdom to earth. His divine, will, intent, and purpose are worth fighting for. Will you get in the fight and become Mighty Men and Women of War? It's now or never! The hour is late. Let him who has ears hear what the Spirit is saying to the church. Maranatha Our Lord come!

Hephzibah, My Delight

Today I would like to encourage you as you embark upon another day's journey with the Lord if you have decided to accept his invitation. Sometimes when I am reading, studying, and medicating on the word of God and just spending time with him I become overwhelmed in the journey. Overwhelmed because walking with Christ is a risk we take and sometimes things don't turn out or go in the way we envisioned them to be. We risk being misunderstood, lonely, and sometimes simply lost, though we know that regardless we must risk all to follow Christ. Once we say yes Lord, we understand that our lives are not our own and we become as the Bond Servant just as Paul became. Anyone that has read or studied the life of the Apostle Paul knows what bond and afflictions he endured for the cause of Christ. I mean at the beginning of Paul's journey he said in Acts 20:22-23 NLT

> *And now I am bound by the Spirit[a] to go to Jerusalem. I don't know what awaits me,²³except that the Holy Spirit tells me in city after city that jail and suffering lie ahead.*

Put it simply, that "Yes Lord, I will serve you. I will lay down my life for you." is easier said than done.

Over the many years of walking with Christ, trust me I have made many mistakes along the way. I have sometimes felt so low that I thought "What's the use? I can't seem to get some things right." But I thank God for repentance and forgiveness that keeps us in right standing with God. A good example of this is Zion. Let's look at God's people in Isaiah 62. At one point in time, they had stopped following the God of their youth and had become forsaken due to sin, but God!

Isaiah 62:1-5

For Zion's sake will I not hold my peace, and for Jerusalem's sake I will not rest, until the righteousness thereof goes forth as brightness, and the salvation thereof as a lamp that burneth.

²And the Gentiles shall see thy righteousness, and all kings thy glory: and thou shalt be called by a new name, which the mouth of the Lord shall name.

³Thou shalt also be a crown of glory in the hand of the Lord, and a royal diadem in the hand of thy God.

⁴Thou shalt no more be termed Forsaken; neither shall thy land any more be termed Desolate: but thou shalt be called Hephzibah, and thy land Beulah: for the Lord delighteth in thee, and thy land shall be married.

⁵For as a young man marrieth a virgin, so shall thy sons marry thee: and as the bridegroom rejoiceth over the bride, so shall thy God rejoice over thee.

Oh, how beautiful of a passage! Hephzibah means 'my delight is in her.' Beulah means 'to be master, to marry.' To take delight is to 'incline to, to bend to, be desired.' I am grateful God has an unfailing love for his Bride, the true church. Though the invaders (sin) had come, the blood of the Lamb covered and was greater. Perhaps the invaders of sin have come upon our land, the land that we are to Christ. Has sin eaten away and is your joy in the Lord diminishing?. Maybe you feel as I that this journey and relationship with Christ challenges us in many ways. Let me encourage you today. Change is here and it's as simple as repenting and asking Christ to help you make that change. It's from the heart all things begin and end. Our hearts must be wholehearted toward Christ and only him. He alone must be the only one to occupy our land. Just as Christ delights in us, so we too will be able to delight in him the same way. He said he delighted in us and he would marry the land. But just like Zion, we must be willing to make change unto a complete surrender of our lives. The Apostle Paul is our great example; he paid a great price but look at the outcome. We are able to read about him and glean in his field because he said "Yes Lord," and was willing to pay the price by laying his life down. Let us join him and leave the great testimony of our lives to those who will follow. I love the lyrics of a song that says "It's the Lord that satisfies." He's the only one that can satisfy us. Money will never do it, a big home will never do it, an important job will never do it. All those things are only a means to an end, and I must say beautiful and wonderful to have. But what happens if we lose all of the above mentioned? Who and what will remain and satisfy? Only Christ alone must be our life.

Someone once said "We see going forward, and we learn looking backwards." I just love that statement and have applied it to my life over many years. That application has given me what some call the big picture. Because what's ahead is so much better and we have figured out along the way what to do and what not to do to avoid the invaders. Look at Christ's big picture in verse 3 of Isaiah 62. *"Thou shall be a crown of glory in the hand of the Lord, a royal diadem."* Oh wow! My friends, that's the big picture. Regardless of what it looks like today, let's look at what we will become! IF we choose to return to the Lord, it will be so worth the hard times! What a mighty God we serve!

As we look out over the landscape our lives individually today, we can all see the things we once could count on to be there are slowly slipping away and everything is on the edge. We are living in unsustainable times and Christ will be the only one who will and is the sustainer of all things. I encourage us today to pause and look over our lives through the eyes of Christ and see if and how much of Christ resides in our heart. Does he truly have full control of our hearts? How much representation of his life is evident in my life? Do I seek God's will when making life decisions? Is it possible we too as Zion have lost the love of our youth for the father? To love him is to obey him. Today is a good day on our journey to make preparation and needed change so that we might delight in Christ as he delights in us. *"Delight thyself in the Lord and he shall give you the desires of your heart."* (Psalms 37:4) Delighting in someone comes from relationship, an inner intimacy of fellowship in good and bad times. In the bad times we go to Christ the Rock that is higher than I. May Christ become all that you need him to be today. Be encouraged in the midst of whatever you are going through and look within and see the indwelling Christ who is your delight.

Beware Of a Cold Love!

One Sunday morning upon arising from good night's sleep I tuned into some of the church programs that were being aired. I stopped as one congregation's worship team was singing. I come from a musical background and love to sing especially when I am singing unto the Lord. Regardless of how my day went or what was going on in my life, when I begin to sing and praise God my spirits were lifted and the joy of the Lord filled my entire being. I have been told by some "Wow Rochelle, I can tell how much you love to sing. Your expressions change. I see the Lord's Spirit in you and I can see it in your smile. I see your joy in your singing and dancing." I must say because his presence has filled my spirit and the love I have for him that I can't help but to rejoice. As the old folks use to say "You can't tell it like I can tell it what the Lord has done for me." Amen and AMEN!

On that particular broadcast as I watched, it appeared like the people and congregation were just going through the motions, just singing about Jesus. Everything seemed cold and flat and expressionless. The joy of the Lord was missing. It was so noticeable to me because it was though I was looking at myself at a period in my relationship with Christ. In that moment I had a flashback of my old life. It was before I actually totally sold out to Christ and laid my life down. I had experienced the exact thing I was witnessing. Oh, I remember the days when I would show up to choir rehearsal, read off the music sheet and just sing the words without a living connection to Christ. I had all the church formality of being a Christian and a singer who carried the title 'I am a Christian' but it was in name only and not life. When a life is joined to Christ, the life will be transformed. The life will take on Christ's life. In the same way that an egg and sperm create a new life when they join, so we should take on a new life when we join with Christ. There was disconnection in my life because I knew of God but not God. I read the pages of the Bible but the words never became living and life unto me. I was living my own life which was sin. It was easy for me to feign, pretend and be affected by a feeling. Sin covers the veils of our heart and affects our hearing. Oh! But praise God! One cold January morning I encountered Christ and made the decision to jump the broom and go all the way. When I committed, Christ met me, took my hand, walked with me through this process and journey. Just as an onion has many layers, you and I have many layers that Christ will peel back but not all at once. As the word says if we be willing and obedient, we will eat the good of the land. (Isaiah 1:19) The key words are willing and obedient. After many years, as Christ has continued to peel back the onion, I began to see what I could not see before. He pulled it back enough for me to see and realize there is a difference between religion and relationship. In my experience religion is like an employer-employee relationship. Religion tells you what to do and how to do it. The hope is that a reward will be given after something has been done well in a certain amount of time. Religion is rooted in rules and regulation. Relationship is based on a covenant of love; it is life based because it is connected to Christ who is our life. Religion is the doing of the things of God without being connected to the God of all things. I sang in the choir but in a lot of cases it was mere formality. Lastly on the subject of religion in my experience, the best example is found in the word of God. Let's look at the Pharisees and Sadducees. The Pharisees were strict in law and tradition. Boy, they had a fit when Jesus healed on the Sabbath day. (Matthew 12:10) They were very devout and zealous and concerned with outward righteousness and the way things appeared. The Sadducees believed in the book of Moses and did not adhere to all the laws of the Pharisees. Like the Pharisees, they were in an uproar when Jesus healed a man's withered hand on the Sabbath. (Luke 6:7) They always tried to find fault and never saw the good, especially if it was not in their traditions. Jesus firmly stated in Mark 7:13 AMP

So, you nullify the [authority of the] word of God [acting as if it did not apply] because of your tradition which you have handed down [through the elders]. And you do many things such as that."

This is what tradition does; it makes the word of God who is Christ the living God of no affect in our lives. This is what happened to me and eventually my love for God grew cold though I yet sang and did the traditional things in church and its formality. I am forever grateful for the day Christ encountered me and the final peel of the onion of my tradition was pulled back. Then I was able to see the error of my ways and the deadness of my spirit. The lyrics to a song 'Oh! the joy that filled my soul' became real to me, once I was transformed from religion to relationship. I promise you, my life has never been the same.

The word says in Matthew 24, one of the signs of the end will be lawlessness. The love of many will wax (or grow) cold. Sin kills. Sin has a deadening affecting on our lives and it will eventually destroy our love for God. If not careful, it will take us from relationship to religion because we believe religion will let us do what we want to do. We falsely believe that sin will be given no penalty. We think "I'm a Christian; God is forgiving." Yes, he is a forgiving God but he warns us also about willful sinning. In Revelations chapter 2 the word of the Lord came to the church Ephesus with a warning, a beware! He said *"I know thy works"* - the doing of the things of God. *"Nevertheless, you have left your first love. Repent and do the first works."* The first works is a relationship with him and not merely works and the things of God. Friends, Christ died for us, not for the things that he blesses us with. We do not have to earn anything from God because he has freely given us all things that pertain unto life and godliness. He desires US, our full love and commitment unto him. If we never ever do a good work is not the issue; he wants us. If that was a factor why is it that John the Baptist never did any great miracles but yet is written as one of the great prophets? Even Christ said there is none greater than John. (Matthew 11:11) May we catch what the Spirit of Christ is saying. If you remember nothing else remember Christ wants YOU and ME; he wants our full love and commitment. Just as he is madly in love with you, he wants you and me to become madly in love with him. As I have said a hundred times, it's a journey. A journey is Christ peeling back every layer of the onion in our lives that he may transform us in into his image and likeliness.

Luke 12:35-36

> *35 "Be dressed for service and keep your lamps burning,36 as though you were waiting for your master to return from the wedding feast. Then you will be ready to open the door and let him in the moment he arrives and knocks.*

You see, it's one thing to be ready to meet Christ but it's another to keep our lamps burning. Hebrews 12:29 tells us Christ is a consuming fire. Let the fire that he is consume our lives with all that he is. Let us be filled with him. I'm sure you have heard the cliché. What consumes your life consumes your time." What are your desires? What affects everything you do? Just as a fire spreads, it consumes everything in its path. Whatever we desire will spread in our lives be it good or bad. Christ must affect us in such a way that all that he is spreads in, through, and out of us. His love for us should be such a consuming love that it affects every decision and everything we do. Our uncompromising love for God will keep our lamps burning. We need a fiery love of passion for Christ; the kind of passion he had for us when he went to the cross. His love for us would not allow him to come down from the cross. Truly it was a passion of love. I am convinced that you and I have as much of Christ as we want. We cannot afford to allow the Spirit of comfortability to find a home in us. Comfortability says "I'm saved. I love God" and we go on our merry way and never seek more of Christ. If not careful, it allows us to only see being a Christian is an escape from hell. The Apostle Paul said *"I press on toward the mark."* (Philippians 3:14). In this case, press means movement. May we never come to a place where we are no longer pressing and allowing Christ to progress in us. Love causes us to press. Psalms says *"Oh taste and see that the Lord is good."* (Psalms 34:8). When we taste and see the goodness of the Lord, it causes us to desire more of him.

On the flip side of things, we must also be careful of a self-love that exceeds our love for Christ. A selfish spirit will override our spirit if we are not careful. A fire not only has a consuming affect but a destroying affect. A fire can be put out; that's why if not careful it can turn into a cold love. A cold love has lost its passion and the desire it once had. A destroying fire destroys and that's what the love of self will do. If we're not careful it will destroy us and separate us from Christ the consuming fire. Let's be as the five wise virgins when the bridegroom came. They were awakened, trimmed their lamps and were ready to go out and meet the bridegroom. Let us keep our lamps trimmed by being filled with Christ always. The light of the Lord within us must shine bright. Willful sinning and compromise will slowly put our light out. Sin plunges us into darkness. Christ said "You are the light of the world." (Matthew 5:14) The children's song says "This little light of mine, I'm going to let it shine." Let your light shine today. Whatever fiery trial comes our way, keep those lights shining. May we not allow our light to be put out by the waters of a cold love. Beware. Let us pray.

Lord, we come humbly today and repent of our cold love toward you. We are sorry for other things consuming us more than you. Open our eyes to see every area in our lives that is not occupied by you. Please come and dismantle any form and spirit of religion within us that masquerades as a true relationship with you. Holy Spirit, teach us to know the difference between religion and relationship. As you teach us let today be a new start of an awakening unto life, the true life that you are. Help us to see and accept that you are all that we need and we are all that you want. Please start a fire in us that can't be contained and controlled. You are that fire, Lord. Come teach us how to rightly love you. Come make us ready to be your beautiful bride as we await you with our lamps trimmed. In Jesus name I pray.

The Bridal Olympian

Today I want to rally and exhort the bride. I love the Olympics and always look forward to watching them on TV with my daughter. Viewing them encourages my spirit to see champions who have no doubt gone through all types of defeats and challenges, standing on top of the podium as winners. Yet even the defeats and challenges they encountered in their journey did not stop them from pushing on. They persevered, especially when it was the hardest. Listening to some of their stories and their agony of defeats is both amazing and inspiring. Many said it was the agony of defeat that pushed them on to become the champions they are today. Some of the gold medalists shared their personal stories of the price they paid to get to the Olympics. My daughter and I love watching ice skating and gymnastics. The gymnast spoke of having to choose to leave home and go live with or near their coaches for training in hopes to one day become world champions. Some spoke of the loneliness of the journey in being away from home, especially on holidays and special occasions, and just the longing for the simplicity of a 'normal' life. They had to choose to forsake family, friends and everything else that would be in the way of them one day becoming the Olympians they desired to become. The families of the Olympians spoke of all the hard sacrifices they also made for their children. They had to learn to have total trust in their children's coaches as well as all those that surround their children and believe they had their child's best interest at heart.

Some of the most heartbreaking stories I heard were from the weeks or days leading up to a big event. The stories that stood out the most were stories when the Olympians had prepared and trained so hard for their big day and events. Weeks before the competition, things did not go the way they had planned. A bad accident during practice prevented them from being a participant. Most of the accidents required extensive surgery that caused great setbacks. Most of what they had worked so hard to learn had to be relearned all over again after surgery and recovery. One common theme that most of the champions spoke of was the challenge of not becoming depressed. That resilience is what caused them to keep moving forward. They envisioned one day seeing themselves on the podium with the gold medal around their neck while their national anthem played on the loudspeaker. The enemy of set-back fueled their passion. They dreamed even more of becoming a champion. While listening I drew the conclusion that from the onset, they had made up their mind to refuse to let obstacles of any kind stop them. Their desire to be a champion far exceeded any challenge they faced regardless of what the challenge was and how fearsome it looked. I think it is simply remarkable to see champions in the making, the go-getters that are not QUITERS. It is amazing what the human body can do by training and shear mental willpower. I am so fascinated by the snowboarders. They do twists and turns way up in the air and still manage to land on both feet. Simply incredible! I think one of the greatest champion stories is Tiger Woods when he won his fifth Masters. After going through many uphill battles and challenges in his life, from family to health issues, he refused to quit. The never-quit factor is what makes champions. He never quit through all of his pain from surgeries. He never quit even though at times he was not even able to put one foot in front of the other. It was his love for the game of golf that continued to drive him through his pain. On Sunday, April 14, 2019, he became the Masters Champ once again. What a great example of being a fighter! That's what I'm talking about- pushing through pain and circumstances, discouragement and difficulties. If these athletes can do it for an earthy crown or prize, my God, what is wrong with us if we can't go after the one that we love? Jesus Christ is our prize. It's something to really think about in reference to where our true allegiance lies.

Let us begin to shed some light on the spiritual athlete and what exactly their requirements are according to the word of God.

I Corinthians 9:24-25

Know ye not that they which run in a race run all, but one receiveth the prize? So run, that ye may obtain. And every man that striveth for the mastery is temperate in all things. Now they do it to obtain a corruptible crown; but we an incorruptible. I therefore so run, not as uncertainly; so fight I, not as one that beateth the air: But I keep under my body, and bring it into subjection: lest that by any means, when I have preached to others, I myself should be a castaway.

This scripture is very revealing and holds many keys to our success in our race. We are running for an incorruptible crown, an eternal crown. This crown does not fade or tarnish. The reward is received on the other side and is not of this world.

All spiritual Olympians, when in training, must be temperate and restrict himself in all things. The way we live is not like everyone else. We must be set apart in our speech, activities and our very life. We will not be saying, doing, and living like those without Christ. We must keep our flesh under at all times and allow the dealings of Christ in our lives to teach and train us. Christ's dealings at times are somewhat challenging and appear to be unfair, yet he knows what each of us need in order to mature our spiritual muscles so we can run the race well. In all things Christ must receive the glory. Just as a coach will train his athletes and stretch them in exercises, always pushing them beyond what they believe they can handle, so Christ does with us. And we come out better for it.

Olympians have to set some rules on themselves. As Paul said, *"I press toward the goal to win the prize of God's heavenly calling in Christ Jesus."* (Philippians 3:14) The Strong concordance says to press is to pursue; by implication. To pursue will require us to stay consistent. This pressing toward our goal to win the race will come with a price. I remember years ago when I told the Lord all I wanted to be was a woman after his own heart. I decided that I was going to go after him regardless of the price. I started setting my alarm clock at 4:00 AM so I could devote time to prayer or studying his word, Sometimes I would just sit and wait in His presence. Often I repeated this practice in the evenings as well. For most of my earlier life I have worked two jobs but I determined I was not going to let that stop me. When I started I discovered I had two enemies-my flesh and the devil. But I was determined. I had many days of failure as well as victories. What I lacked was consistency. As any Olympian, I kept on in spite of my failures and days when I felt like giving up. I wanted to get back on track. I had set my goal and didn't want to fall short. It was difficult, but nonetheless, I continued to pursue and as I did I began to see results in my relationship. Communion with the father began to slowly grow. I began to see my spiritual muscles flex and strengthen. His voice became easier and easier for me to discern. His life began to grown in me. His life that had started out as a tiny seed began to grow. The more it did, the more my two enemies began to grow weaker and weaker. After many years it's no different. I am still rising early, some days staying up late to pursue the one that I love, the one that is the prize. I made up my mind a long time ago I'm going for the *"Well done thy good and faithful servant."* (Luke 19:17) I would hate to hear just the word WELL! when I stand before the father on judgment day.

I say all that to say as the scripture tells us in Revelations 3:21

To him that overcomes will I grant to sit with me in my throne, even as I also overcame, and am set down with my father in his throne.

God is coming back for an overcoming Bride, one that has conquered the spoils of war. One that has dethroned the love of self. Victory is sweet. I never really thought about that until one day I was listening to sports on the news and they began to talk about the millions they were paying their quarterback because they wanted a WINNING TEAM.

Money was not a factor. All the owners and coaches want is a winning team. They want that Super Bowl championship ring on their finger AT ALL COST. I immediately began to look at that scenario from a spiritual perspective. What are we the church, the bride, willing to give up to become a spiritual Olympian and Olympian bride? Can we as the energizer battery, take a licking and keep on ticking? Are we willing to fast and pray and make a serious commitment that, regardless of the price, we want a winning team? Now that is food for thought. It is something that must be considered as we determine to become over-comers in order to reign with Christ. That means we will be confronted with hard trials and situations. At times it may even appear that Christ doesn't care what we are going though. We may feel like he is not there at all. I know that is rough; it's been a way of life for me too. But Christ is always present. It's like someone once said, "When you're taking a test, it seems the teacher is not present but she is watching you. The teacher is still in the room though she cannot help you take or pass the exam." My friends, Christ will train all of us by a hard path. We simply must decide to be winners and taste the sweetness of victory by remaining resilient and persistent.

Today we have to make some decisions if we are going to be spiritual Olympians for Christ. If we determine to go all the way to the finish line without entanglement in the affairs of this life, we must decide to live right. I love what a man of God once said, "You can't live wrong and pray right" LOL! It's so true. I'm not sure where you are in the race or even what type of race you are running. Let me encourage you. If you are running for the incorruptible crown, don't give up. Don't be distracted or discouraged. *"Run the race that is set before you, looking to Jesus. the author and finisher of your faith."* (Hebrews 12:2) You can do it. Let us run, Olympians.

Prayer Changes Everything for the Bride

Oh! How I love the story of Hannah! I no doubt know that somewhere in our lives we are experiencing or living her story. I am sure a prototype of her life resonates with each of us in some way. I know it resonates with me and has many times over along this journey. If you are not familiar with her story in I Samuel 1 and 2 I encourage you read it. As you make yourselves familiar with her story, I assure you, you won't be disappointed.

Hannah and Peninnah were wives of the same husband Elkanah. Hannah was barren and full of sorrow as she longed for a son. Peninnah was fruitful in her womb and had children. Peninnah became Hannah's adversary. She provoked and vexed Hannah because her womb was shut. To be barren was an embarrassment, in those days, and Hannah was in deep anguish. I can't imagine living in the same house with an adversary being married to the same man. However, Hannah was Elkanah's favorite and he loved her. Year by year Hannah went up to the temple of the Lord, provoked by the taunting of Peninnah. Elkanah was concerned and asked, "Why are you weeping, not eating and your heart grieved? Am I not better to thee than ten sons?" Oh! I'm sure he was, but the desire of Hannah's heart was to have a son. Hannah went in the temple to pray in much distress as she poured out her heart to God. In I Samuel 1:11 we see that Hannah made a vow to God.

"O Lord of host. If thou will indeed look on the affliction of thine hand maid, and remember me and not forget thine handmaid, but wilt give unto thine handmaid a man child, then I will give him unto the Lord all the days of his life, and there shall no razor come upon his head." Hannah vowed to God from the beginning her son would be a Nazarite, which means he would be consecrated and separated unto a lifelong purpose.

That day settled it for Hannah. She laid her all on the altar and poured out her heart to the Lord. Vows have power and hold much weight, both to the one that made the vow and also to the one on the receiving end. God is and has always been about covenant, which is a binding contract between two people based on serious ramifications if either party breaks their end of the deal.

Eli the priest saw Hannah praying but could not hear what she prayed. Her lips were moving but no words could be heard. At first Eli thought she had been drinking and was drunk! Hannah said, *"Oh! Count me not thine handmaid for a daughter of Belial."* (I Samuel 1:16)

Belial means wicked, unprofitable. Hannah was a godly woman, and the meaning of her name is Grace. Hannah had a grace on her life that set her apart. She was nothing like Peninnah. The distinction is so clear as it should be when it comes to God's people and the people who belong to Belial, the wicked one. Eli told Hannah to go in peace and said that God would grant her petition. When we petition God, we are asking God for something with our heart surrendered in humble submission. I am not sure of the days, weeks, or months that Hannah petitioned God before Eli told her that her prayers would be answered. But we can see that God did finally grant her request. How good is God? She asks for a man child and that's exactly what God gave her. I believe when Hannah's heart lined up with God's eternal will, he answered. She vowed, "If you give me a child I will give him back to you." How beautiful! God's plan was to replace the priesthood through Samuel, Hannah's child. This has helped me to see and understand the ways of God in my own life. Many times, I have prayed for things for a very long time and it seemed that God would never answer. At times I would even wonder, "God, do you hear or care at all?" But I can now see that prayers are answered according to God eternal will and plan for our lives.

I have seen some prayers answered and some I am yet praying and petitioning God for. Just like Hannah, I will pray for weeks or years, as long as is necessary. God is faithful. Truly prayer changes things, just as it did for Hannah. The word says *"My house shall be called a house of prayer."* (Matthew 21:13). That means you and I as the temple of God, should be filled with prayer and it should be a life style. We should not only be praying to receive from God but also because we want to know him and become more deeply and intimately acquainted with him. The bride must become a house of prayer. We must be committed to stick with it until we see, like Hannah, our requests and petitions granted to us according to God's will. But even more than that, we see his eternal will come to pass in our lives. We were created for God.

Just like Hannah, we have some adversaries. Peninnah was Hanna's adversary. I'm sure Hannah also faced adversaries of discouragement, doubt and sorrow. But thank God, the day came when her adversaries were put to flight and no more. The day she conceived and gave birth to her son Samuel every adversary was checked! Game over! Christ has conquered! Now, I am not sure what adversaries you are facing today. Perhaps you too are barren; perhaps your adversary is a sickness, disease, unemployment, finances, a broken relationship with God, your family or whatever. The good news is Christ is a God who hears and answers prayer. I pray your adversaries are not vexing you as Peninnah vexed Hannah, but if so, guess what? The table always turns. Be encouraged. May we see the encouraging word the Lord gave to Moses in Exodus 14:13

> *And Moses said unto the people, Fear ye not, stand still, and see the salvation of the LORD, which he will shew to you today: for the Egyptians whom ye have seen today, ye shall see them again no more forever.*

I love this word. Christ put the smack down! The enemies they had seen that day they would see no more. I believe it's no different for us. We just must be willing to stay consistent in our relationship and pursuit of God and his will for our lives. Stay consistent in our prayer petitions and become the house of prayer that aligns with the will of God. Don't give up. Remember God will always have the last word and the last laugh.

After Hannah received her long-awaited son, she had a prayer and a song for her Lord. Oh, that's too good not to share here. I just love it and every time I read it, it makes me want to shout! And sometimes I do! I hope you enjoy it as much as I do and are blessed by it as you are waiting for your petition to be answered and your adversaries to be dethroned. Stay consistent in prayer and as one of my mottos says "We don't back down; we pray up! Halleluiah!

Then Hannah prayed and said:

> *"My heart rejoices in the Lord;*
> *in the Lord my horn[a] is lifted high.*
> *My mouth boasts over my enemies,*
> *for I delight in your deliverance.*
> [2] *"There is no one holy like the Lord;*
> *there is no one besides you;*
> *there is no Rock like our God.*
> [3] *"Do not keep talking so proudly*
> *or let your mouth speak such arrogance,*
> *for the Lord is a God who knows,*
> *and by him deeds are weighed.*
> [4] *"The bows of the warriors are broken,*
> *but those who stumbled are armed with strength.*
> [5] *Those who were full hire themselves out for food,*

but those who were hungry are hungry no more.
She who was barren has borne seven children,
but she who has had many sons pines away.
⁶"The Lord brings death and makes alive;
he brings down to the grave and raises up.
⁷ The Lord sends poverty and wealth;
he humbles and he exalts.
⁸He raises the poor from the dust
and lifts the needy from the ash heap;
he seats them with princes
and has them inherit a throne of honor.
"For the foundations of the earth are the Lord's;
on them he has set the world.
⁹He will guard the feet of his faithful servants,
but the wicked will be silenced in the place of darkness.
"It is not by strength that one prevails;
¹⁰those who oppose the Lord will be broken.
The Most High will thunder from heaven;
the Lord will judge the ends of the earth.
"He will give strength to his king
and exalt the horn of his anointed."

I Samuel 2:1-10

I pray we can see everything has its origins, its alpha, in prayer. Prayer is like the dark room that develops the picture and brings it into view. All things are first spiritual before they are physical. Prayerlessness is for losers; they will take the big "L." Complacent people will never win.

There is another prayer I am drawn to and have prayed often. It's the prayer of Daniel chapter 9.

²In the first year of his reign I Daniel understood by books the number of the years, where of the word of the Lord came to Jeremiah the prophet, that he would accomplish seventy years in the desolations of Jerusalem.

³And I set my face unto the Lord God, to seek by prayer and supplications, with fasting, and sackcloth, and ashes:

⁴And I prayed unto the Lord my God, and made my confession, and said, O Lord, the great and dreadful God, keeping the covenant and mercy to them that love him, and to them that keep his commandments;

⁵We have sinned, and have committed iniquity, and have done wickedly, and have rebelled, even by departing from thy precepts and from thy judgments:

⁶Neither have we hearkened unto thy servants the prophets, which spake in thy name to our kings, our princes, and our fathers, and to all the people of the land.

⁷O Lord, righteousness belongeth unto thee, but unto us confusion of faces, as at this day; to the men of Judah, and to the inhabitants of Jerusalem, and unto all Israel, that are near, and that are far off, through all the countries whither thou hast driven them, because of their trespass that they have trespassed against thee.

⁸O Lord, to us belongeth confusion of face, to our kings, to our princes, and to our fathers, because we have sinned against thee.

⁹To the Lord our God belong mercies and forgivenesses, though we have rebelled against him;

¹⁰Neither have we obeyed the voice of the Lord our God, to walk in his laws, which he set before us by his servants the prophets.

¹¹Yea, all Israel have transgressed thy law, even by departing, that they might not obey thy voice; therefore the curse is poured upon us, and the oath that is written in the law of Moses the servant of God, because we have sinned against him.

12And he hath confirmed his words, which he spake against us, and against our judges that judged us, by bringing upon us a great evil: for under the whole heaven hath not been done as hath been done upon Jerusalem.

13As it is written in the law of Moses, all this evil is come upon us: yet made we not our prayer before the Lord our God, that we might turn from our iniquities, and understand thy truth.

14Therefore hath the Lord watched upon the evil, and brought it upon us: for the Lord our God is righteous in all his works which he doeth: for we obeyed not his voice.

15And now, O Lord our God, that hast brought thy people forth out of the land of Egypt with a mighty hand, and hast gotten thee renown, as at this day; we have sinned, we have done wickedly.

16O Lord, according to all thy righteousness, I beseech thee, let thine anger and thy fury be turned away from thy city Jerusalem, thy holy mountain: because for our sins, and for the iniquities of our fathers, Jerusalem and thy people are become a reproach to all that are about us.

17Now therefore, O our God, hear the prayer of thy servant, and his supplications, and cause thy face to shine upon thy sanctuary that is desolate, for the Lord's sake.

18O my God, incline thine ear, and hear; open thine eyes, and behold our desolations, and the city which is called by thy name: for we do not present our supplications before thee for our righteousness's, but for thy great mercies.

19O Lord, hear; O Lord, forgive; O Lord, hearken and do; defer not, for thine own sake, O my God: for thy city and thy people are called by thy name.

Did you catch it? Daniel's prayer is relevant for our time as I see the state and condition of our nation as did Daniel. I see our nation imploding quickly. At that time Israel was in captivity because of sin. They had national transgression which brought about calamities all because of sin. I see a resemblance, don't you? There is much calamity in our nation. A nation that once was God fearing, had safe borders to protect its citizens, freedom of speech is being blinded by sin. Truth and honesty have all been trodden under foot. Even worse are the parallels of our nation alongside Sodom and Gomorrah. The cities' wickedness has become proverbial. Sodom was vile and had vile affections as we see in Romans 1:26. Out of the name Sodom comes the word sodomy. The people prided themselves in unnatural uncleanness and sexual sins and were destroyed. They were lovers of self and prideful according to Ezekiel 16:49 AMP

[49] Behold, this was the sin of your sister Sodom: she and her daughters (outlying cities) had arrogance, abundant food, and careless ease, but she did not help the poor and needy.

While all the sin and perversion were going on, thank God there was a man name Abraham, A **PRAYING MAN,** holy and blameless before God. Abraham knew that sin would destroy and God would eventually judge and unleash his wrath. In Genesis 18:17-33, the Lord himself came down to see the situation in Sodom and Gomorrah because the CRY OF SIN WAS SO GREAT. My God! Sin has a cry that goes directly to the throne of God. Though people try and hide their sins, it's impossible. Sin has a cry and nothing is hidden from God. The people of Sodom and Gomorrah were having a good time and were caught unaware. I'm reminded of the Laodicean church when Christ knocked on their door. The scripture says Abraham drew near and began to intercede and ask the Lord "If you find 50 righteous in the city, will you not destroy? The Lord for the sake of 50 righteous men said he would not destroy the city. Abraham interceded down to ten righteous in the city, but sadly they were not to be found. Yet God said he would not destroy the righteous with the wicked. He allowed Abraham's relatives to leave town before the destruction began. God is a merciful God.

I'm afraid to say that what I am witnessing in our nations has surpassed Sodom and Gomorrah. This PRIDE agenda is being promoted and accepted in our nation, destroying the family and our children. Sin is viewed lightly. Sinful men love dark rather than light, a lie rather than the truth. These things are not to be so. There is no fear of the Lord in our nation and because God has been longsuffering many think they are getting away with sin. They think they are safe, sin doesn't matter and God will not act. Nothing could be further from the truth.

Here is my question for us as a nation; is there a cry of sin coming up to our ears? Is there a cry of evil coming up to our ears that causes us to listen and humble ourselves before God? The Lord pointed out to me that whenever the Israelites knew they had sin and were in trouble, they called Solomon assemblies. These were special times of prayer, sanctification and fasting because of sin and trouble. It was a time of repentance and contrition. I'm sure it happens in our world today, but not as often as it should.

Getting back to the prayer of Daniel, we can see that's exactly what he did. "He humbled himself and said we have sinned; we have rebelled and we have confusion of faces." (Daniel 9:7) Boy, can I relate to that. When we look out over this nation, everyone seems confused! What happened? What is going on? We need a Republican president, we need a Democratic president, we need a third-party candidate. REALLY? NO! What we need is to humble ourselves, repent and turn back to God. (II Chronicles 7:14) We need to confess we have sinned. We have transgressed the Lord's commandments and we need get right. Christ in you and me is the hope of glory. Our hope is not found in a political party. That type of thinking really is confusion. Lord helps us. Can we not see our need for God? The bride must awaken and arise. She must become the vessel that God uses just as Daniel became the Lord's vessel and allowed the eternal will and plan of God to come forth.

I realize I am speaking very candidly in this journal. I do so under the direction of the Lord. We must wake up and see that fence-sitting time is over. Either we are going to get all the way out to God or not. Today is the day of decision; it's not on one day and off the next. We must remain with God regardless of how hard it gets. I can tell you now, it won't get any easier because we are in the fullness of time and God is bringing all things to completion.

Awaken Oh Bride! Get out to God. God is not Baptist, Methodist, Pentecostal, Unitarian, or anything else. He is not denominational. He is God and he is relational. How about today we decide we hear the cry of sin in our ears? Let's drop to our knees and begin to pray and allow Christ to have his rightful place first in us the church and then to the nation and nations of the earth. May we become one with him even if that means going it alone. Trust me, the narrow way is never crowded. Let us pray.

Heavenly father, I ask today in the name of Jesus that you would humble us so that we see from whence we have fallen. Soften our hearts that we may repent and return. I pray, Lord, that you remove veils that cover our eyes so we can see clearly and unstop our ears so that we may hear. I pray that the fear of God will return to our hearts and nation. I pray that we will see sin as you do and come to hate it. Give us courage to step out and trust you even if that means stepping out alone. I ask that you would encounter your people in a mighty way. I ask that you would visit them in dreams and visions and however you need to make yourself real to them. Help us to see the traps of the enemy and uncover all his deception in our lives. Please push back all darkness in our lives and remove everything that keeps us from seeing you. I pray that you bless everyone that reads these words today. Father, you know their every need and situation. Father, speak to them in a way that only you can, teach them to walk closely with you. May they realize you love them more than they can ever know. Thanks in advance Father. In Jesus' name I pray. Amen.

Know my friend, you are loved beyond measure.

Vows

In the last journal we saw the power and significance of a vow. We learned about the vow Hannah made to her Lord. Throughout the scripture we see the importance of vows. I believe those who truly pledge vows and keep them are those who are serious about their commitments.

The Smith Bible dictionary defines a vow as a solemn promise made to God to perform or to abstain from performing a certain thing. Vows are necessary and significant in the lives of the believer. I believe God expects them, and it reminds me of a slogan "Put your money where your mouth is." If we are really serious about anything, primarily our commitment to God, we will pledge vows in hopes to keeping them. The vows will become the primary focus of our lives.

Job 22:27

You will pray to him, and he will hear you, and you will fulfill your vows.

Jacob also realized the power of the vow in Genesis 31:13.

[13] I am the God who appeared to you at Bethel, [a] the place where you anointed the pillar of stone and made your vow to me. Now get ready and leave this country and return to the land of your birth.

As I've written before growing up in church as a pastor's kid for me entailed singing in choirs. I recall when church used to have a choir day. Different churches from the surrounding area would send their choirs to participate. Sometimes one person would represent a choir as some churches were small and did not have a lot of youth in them. There was a gentleman who would always sing the same song "I Made a Vow to the Lord." At that time, I wondered why he always sang the same song and I wasn't quite sure of the song in reference to making vows. However, as I grew and became more personal with the Lord, I realized I had made a few vows myself in ignorance, not knowing what all the making of a vow required, as well as the seriousness of keeping vows.

The book of Ecclesiastes shows the mind of Christ in reference to vows.

Ecclesiastes' 5:4-5

⁴When you make a vow or a pledge to God, do not put off paying it; for God takes no pleasure in fools [who thoughtlessly mock Him]. Pay what you vow.⁵It is better that you should not vow than that you should vow and not pay.

The Ultimate Bible Dictionary also says vows are voluntary expressions of devotion usually fulfilled after some conditions had been met. Simply put, vows are words of commitment. God commits himself to us and we pledge ourselves to one another. I see now that when I was younger, I had made many commitments to the Lord. I pledged myself to him and his will for my life but never followed though until after many years. I now understand what the word says. "It is better to not vow than to vow and not pay because it is foolish." (Ecclesiastes 5:5) Once again, I thank God for his mercy unto me over the many years in my journey. At times I have traveled in a wayward fashion, but Christ called me back. I love what David said *"His gentleness has made me great."* (Psalms 18:35) Amen!

Whether we realize it or not, we all made a vow if we accepted Christ into our heart as our Lord and Savior. In essence, we were saying, "I give myself to you, Lord." It's no different in natural marriage.

The traditional marriage was founded on vows. In my view, vows in marriage pour from a deep heartfelt love. You are pouring your whole being into the other person as you are on your way to becoming one. A heart is committed and dedicated to the other and both share a love that only wants to serve, love and protect the other. So the vow says "I give myself to thee."

Upon my research, I found some interesting facts about marriage The statistics are very disheartening in light of the meaning of marriage and how lightly vows are taken. From Christianity.com the average length of marriage in US is 8.2 years and somewhere between 40 to 50% of marriage end in divorce. Yikes! According to a 2014 study by Baylor University the divorce rate of those who call themselves Christians is HIGHER than for non-Christians! OMG! That's shocking and sadly unbelievable. Where have we gone wrong? I firmly believe that no marriage, regardless of the vows, will ever last if their relationship with Christ is not in good standing. You can only love someone to the degree they know God because God is love. God is love! Let me say it again - God is love! The word says to know him is to love him. (I John 4:16) Once again, our first vow is to God when we accepted him. If we have strayed from keeping that vow then no doubt any other vow we make will be broken. I do understand that in some cases due to violence and others situation that cause harm, divorce in a natural marriage may happen.

Marriage and making vows are about being separated unto the one you love. I am not sure it's understood that our vow to the Lord is about commitment to him. He will never hurt or harm us. We must be willing to stay committed even when it's hard and we do not always understand. Love is the bond that will hold us together with the Lord. I often think of the ultimate sacrifice the Lord paid for you and for me. His vow to us is, *"He that believes in me shall not perish but have everlasting life."* (John 3:16) *"All that come to me I will in no wise cast out."* (John 6:37) He proved his vow. He made a vow even to ones he knew would never love him. Oh, what commitment. He is our perfect example of love, to love and be loved.

Let us remember today if we choose to become the Lord's bride we must consider our vows and understand there are consequences if we fail to keep them. A covenant in marriage is not forced upon anyone as it is based on love. Christ never forces himself on anyone to love him and neither should we. Vows require commitment and responsibility on both sides. Let take a peek at what brother James tells us.

James 5:12

But above all things, my brethren, swear not, neither by heaven, neither by the earth, neither by any other oath: but let your yea be yea; and your nay, nay; lest ye fall into condemnation.

In closing, if anyone desires to renew their vows with the Lord let our yea be yea. That means "Yes, Lord, regardless of what I do not see or understand I commit myself to you because I know you love me and know what's best for me." In this season of time, Christ is looking for a wholehearted bride, a people that will commit fully to him and be his and his alone. It's a journey of becoming one with him. Maybe you're a person that can say, "I at one time broke my vow because I was ignorant, but I want to recommit today." Know that the Lord your God waits for your wholehearted "Yes!" He is ready to be all you need and he himself will never leave or forsake you. Say Yes! It will be the best yes you will ever make. I am a witness and can testify. I'm still here; he's still here with me. He's kept his vow! And with his help I will keep mine. Forever be blessed by the presence of the Lord and be encouraged my, beautiful friends. You are never alone.

The Midnight Bride Cry

Let us be glad and rejoice and give honor to him for the marriage of the Lamb is come and his wife hath made herself ready. *Rev 19:7*

Amen!

As a little girl one of my favorite fairy tales was Cinderella. The movie always kept me on the edge of my seat in suspense. I wondered if stories like hers could ever come true. Could it even be real? Of course, not real in the fact of being a stepchild hated by her siblings, dressed in rags, and forced to be a housemaid. God forbid! But real in reference to there really being a charming Prince and a real Bride where everything falls in perfect place in the right time, in the right moment. In the fairytale there is a pumpkin that turn into a carriage and Cinderella's clothes are changed from rages to a beautiful gown in an instant. Her enemy was midnight as everything would change. In the end her charming prince found her and they lived happily ever after.

For the church, midnight is very significant time in its symbolism of the hour in which we now live. Midnight (Mid-Nit) means middle of the night. It is the shift between one day to another, and it happens while most of us are sleeping. I do realize that some of us work the night shift, but in general, midnight usually comes while people sleep. Midnight also represents the darkness before dawn. Many Biblical things seem to happen at midnight. In Acts 16:22-25 Paul and Silas are in a Roman jail, beaten with stripes. They began to sing praises unto their God at midnight. The prison gates were opened unto them.

Midnight is also represented as a time of rest but at the same time it is a time when we can easily be caught off guard. We always need to be aware of the spiritual climate of the days and times in which we are living. By watching and praying, we do not have to be caught off guard. It's no different than a natural wedding. A date and time are set. A schedule of events month by month is followed so that the big day will go off smoothly. Details to bring the big event to life are being put together. Invitations are sent out to family and friends. The excitement grows as each day brings the bride closer and closer to her big day. For the betrothed Bride we are getting our spiritual houses in order; we are inviting the groom Christ Jesus to come make us ready. Our excitement as the church should be ever increasing and growing because the Lord says in Luke 21:25-28 NLT

> [25] *"And there will be strange signs in the sun, moon, and stars. And here on earth the nations will be in turmoil, perplexed by the roaring seas and strange tides.* [26] *People will be terrified at what they see coming upon the earth, for the powers in the heavens will be shaken.* [27] *Then everyone will see the Son of Man[a] coming on a cloud with power and great glory.* [b][28] *So when all these things begin to happen, stand and look up, for your salvation is near!"*

Can we not see the signs? The perplexity, calamity and darkness in our nation? Oh! But the Lord says *"Look up for your redemption draws nigh."* (Luke 21:28) Hallelujah! This should cause us to be excited, looking for the one we love in expectancy. We know that there is still yet much to be fulfilled on the earth, but each day brings us closer to Christ's return. This delay is giving us time to prepare. As the natural bride sets everything in order, so we too must make sure our hearts are decorated with his beauty and life. We make ourselves spotless and without blemish. We crown our heads with his righteousness. We light our lamps to be ready for his return. This type of expectation will keep the bride from being caught off guard in the midnight hour. The Lord is so gracious and wants to get his word out to his people. That is why I am only one of many writing this type of book. The Lord desires that no one be caught off guard. Time has a way of being a thief in our lives. But we must be awakened to the times we are living and move accordingly. We can no longer be an ostrich with our heads buried in the sand. We must prepare for that midnight cry! *"Behold the bridegroom comes, go ye out to meet him."* (Matthew 25:6) I have come to realize that seeing things from my own eyes instead of through the lens of Christ has in times past set me on the wrong course. I had to be willing to see and accept things as they are and not the way I wanted to see them. We are in the midnight hour and God is coming back for his church without wrinkle or blemish.

There was a church in the book of Revelation, the last book of the Bible, called the Laodicean church. (Revelations 3:14-22) The people in the Laodicean church were looking at themselves through the lenses of their own eyes and heart. Man does not see as God sees. In their eyes they were rich, increased with goods, and had everything they needed. They had everything but Christ! That's why he told them *"Buy of me gold tried in the fire."* (Revelation 3:18) They lacked relationship with him and didn't have the love for him they should have had. Christ divinely interrupted them. They could not see because they had veils that covered their eyes. But in the eyes of God, they were wretched, miserable, poor, blind, and naked. He rebuked and chastened them because he loved them as he loves us. He told them, *"Behold I stand at the door and knock."* (Revelation 3:20) He's knocking on the door of the church, his bride, today. No bride wants to come down the aisle to meet her groom in a filthy, torn gown looking miserable. We are in a midnight hour and God is knocking on the door of our hearts. The darkest hour is coming. Are we ready? Let us become the prepared bride. Ask the Holy Spirit to touch our hearts and renew our dedication to him. At a wedding ceremony, the pastor raises his arms to indicate that we should rise for the bride. But our bridegroom will say *"Behold the bridegroom comes. Arise and meet him!"* (Matthew 25:6)

 *Tie the Knot*

I remember when I was a little girl, going to church was a part of our lifestyle. We lived in the country in Kingdom City, Missouri and my family had a church called Old Richland. I always remember seeing all the familiar faces and hearing the screeching of the wooden floors as everyone walked about. I remember a song that was sung at times either by them or other choirs that would come sing. "Blest be the ties that bind" was the title. Of course, when I was younger, I did not know the meaning of the song. As kids, my siblings and I were usually tired and ready for the service to be over before it even got started. As I have come to grow in the Lord, I now understand the lyrics of the song The words are beautiful and full of meaning. As I researched the hymnal from Timeless Truth Library, I found that John Fawcett was the published author in 1782. I believe the lyrics are beautiful and befitting for this journal.

Blest be the tie that binds
Our hearts in Christian love;
The fellowship of kindred minds
Is like to that above.

Before our father's throne,
We pour our ardent prayers;
Our fears, our hopes, our aims are one,
Our comforts, and our cares.

We share our mutual woes,
Our mutual burdens bear;
And often for each other flows
The sympathizing tear.

When we asunder part,
It gives us inward pain;
But we shall still be joined in heart,
And hope to meet again.

To tie has several meanings from the Webster dictionary - to fasten, attach, or close by means of a tie, to form a knot or bow in, to place or establish in relationship, to unite in marriage. In society there is a common term used when people are getting married which is 'I am going to tie the knot.' I love research and digging into things for the origin. I find so many intersecting and valuable facts that in some cases set a foundation for many of our choices and decisions in life. Interestingly, I found an article in the Readers Digest with the origins of 'Tie the Knot' and its meaning. It is an ancient Celtic practice that bands couples together with a piece of cloth tied around their hands.

Hand-fasting usually happens outdoors when couples say their vows in addition to the official ceremony. The most popular method is to tie a knot for each vow. Couples are able to keep the cloth at the conclusion of the practice as a reminder of what they promised. During the Middle Ages, hand-fasting was typically part of the betrothal or engagement period in order to further bond the couple before the official wedding. Wow! Tie the knot is a symbol of bonding and a reminder to stay committed to their vows. I love the aspect that hand-fasting was a part of the betrothal or engagement period. As I have always believed and stated everything starts from the inside out. So actually, the commitment and bonding began in engagement and not actually per say at the altar. The ceremony was an outward showing of an inward act of two hearts already bonded, committed, tied, and connected. I'd say that's shouting ground!

Now that we have laid a foundation, let's look at it from a spiritual stand point. What does it mean for us to be tied and united to Christ first and then to one another? I Corinthians 6:17 NLT says "But the person who is joined to the Lord is one spirit with him." Those joined are in union with Christ. Union is oneness of thought, will, and intent. We no longer live but Christ lives in us and guides our every decision. Siamese twins are a great illustration of being joined. One can't go without the other; they must be in full agreement with each other to be successful in their life. They are closely bound together; all they have is each other. One heart. That's the tie and bond in a marriage relationship naturally and spiritually. Once vows are declared and the knot tied, the individual lives are joined in union. The two vow to become one in thought, will and intention. Love is the foundation and life of any relationship. No one in their right mind would every force anyone to love them. Neither does God. He gave his only begotten son to die for us even though he knew not all would love him or ever accept him. That is ultimate love and commitment. In our betrothal journey with the Lord, he is offering his hand to us, to become one and joined with him in heart. He is a gentleman and will never force his way in or upon us. He wants our heart to be totally tied to his. He will not marry a halfhearted bride; neither will he fully give himself to her.

In Colossians 2:2 the Apostle Paul extorts us.

I want them to be encouraged and knit together by strong ties of love. I want them to have complete confidence that they understand God's mysterious plan, which is Christ himself.

He encourages his converts to be knit together by ties of love to one another. As they tie themselves together, they have confidence, and they will understand Christ himself. They will come into a deep knowledge of him as he unveils himself. But first it all comes from having a bond. So it is with us; the more completely we give our heart to the Lord, the more he unveils himself in love and relationship. Just beautiful! I am sure you have experienced a new relationship, whether in friend or marriage. As times goes on and you think you have come to

know the person pretty well, you may be surprised when they begin to unveil or show a new side of themselves that you didn't know. Think of it as uncovering the beauty of a person like a new flower being opened in the sun. You may think to yourself, "Wow! I like that about him!" or "Why didn't they tell me?" More than likely it was a level of trust that was necessary and growing. The trust you began to allow encourages new revelations. When you and I feel comfortable enough to let the door of our hearts open little wider, things began to change. That's the way it is in our relationship with our heavenly father. When we begin to show interest in him and make room for him in our heart and life relationships, he reveals so many facets of who he is. I absolutely love that about him. In the Song of Songs, I love the cry of the Shulamite women because she said "Draw me and I will come running" I have followed her example in my life and it has paid off. When we ask him to draw us, that's his signal and gives him the consent to come a little closer. One thing the Lord told me years ago is this; "Rochelle, he who is hungry will eat and he who is thirsty will drink." He was letting me know if you are satisfied, you will never ask the Lord to draw you, fill you, teach you how to love him. That means you are satisfied. But my friend, there is always more in and of God than we will ever experience. Ask him for more! Never be satisfied! Complacency should never be allowed to exist in our life and journey. If we choose to be complacent, Christ will not violate our free will. He will never force himself into a deeper relationship. However, I must add, if we get to a place where we no longer see our need for God, we are on dangerous ground and not holy ground. Why do I say that? Because we will be depending on the arm of the flesh, meaning our strength, human will, human understanding, human confidence. The word says to put no confidence in the flesh. (Philippians 3:3) I call flesh glorified dirt. We were made from the dust of the earth and became glorified when Christ the glorified one came to live in us. As I said earlier, love is a great motivator and God gave his son out of love. He will pursue us all because of love, but he will never take away our free will of choice.

In closing let us look at Hosea Chapter 11:1-5

1 When Israel was a child, then I loved him, and called my son out of Egypt.

2 As they called them, so they went from them: they sacrificed unto Baalim, and burned incense to graven images.

3 I taught Ephraim also to go, taking them by their arms; but they knew not that I healed them.

4 I drew them with cords of a man, with bands of love: and I was to them as they that take off the yoke on their jaws, and I laid meat unto them.

This passage is so beautiful! Even when God's people had gone astray, he drew them with cords of love. God is a covenant-keeping God. His vows are etched in stone and the depths of his love cannot be comprehended by us.

Romans 8:35-39 NLT

35 Can anything ever separate us from Christ's love? Does it mean he no longer loves us if we have trouble or calamity, or are persecuted, or hungry, or destitute, or in danger, or threatened with death? 36 (As the Scriptures say, "For your sake we are killed every day; we are being slaughtered like sheep.") 37 No, despite all these things, overwhelming victory is ours through Christ, who loved us.

38 And I am convinced that nothing can ever separate us from God's love. Neither death nor life, neither angels nor demons, [p] neither our fears for today nor our worries about tomorrow—not even the powers of hell can separate us from God's love. 39 No power in the sky above or in the earth below—indeed, nothing in all creation will ever be able to separate us from the love of God that is revealed in Christ Jesus our Lord.

Somebody shout with me! Look at what our Lord is saying. Nothing can separate us from God's love. Can we not be a people who will choose to tie the knot forever with our Lord and walk on a journey of becoming one with him now and forever more? As I leave,

I want to say. "Blest be the tie that binds." Let us be bound to Christ and one another.

Deuteronomy 11:18

[18]*"So commit yourselves wholeheartedly to these words of mine. Tie them to your hands and wear them on your forehead as reminders.*[19]*Teach them to your children. Talk about them when you are at home and when you are on the road, when you are going to bed and when you are getting up.*[20]*Write them on the doorposts of your house and on your gates,*[21]*so that as long as the sky remains above the earth, you and your children may flourish in the land the Lord swore to give your ancestors.*

Forever tie the word of the Lord to your heart. Be knitted and joined in love with him and one another. Have a wonderful journey!

Searching for Love in all the Wrong Places

I am sure you have heard the phrase "Searching for love in all the wrong places." Place and places are a very general terms in their meaning but opens up a wide range of what can be considered as a place. One thing for sure I have come to know, and that is God is love. I have always said "God is a package deal. When you find him you find all you need"

Whoever is searching for love can find it in God.

Over many years of my life, I have been intrigued with the book Song of Solomon and the Shulamite women. I've written about her previously but I want to look at the story from a different angle in this journal. The book, which some reference as the Song of Songs, is a beautiful love song of our father the bridegroom to his beautiful bride the church. When reading about King Solomon's life in the scripture we can see at one time had many wives.

I Kings 11:1, 4

"But King Solomon loved many foreign women, as well as the daughter of Pharaoh: women of the Moabites, Ammonites, Edomites, Sidonians, and Hittites. As Solomon grew old, his wives turned his heart after other gods, and his heart was not fully devoted to the LORD his God".

I am not sure if King Solomon was looking for love in the wrong places or not. One thing is for sure; to be involved with anyone or anything that turns our hearts away from the Lord is a BAD PLACE. One thing I must trumpet here and now. Though there will always be many virgins there will only be one bride that Christ will marry. Christ requires a bride that is totally and wholeheartedly committed to him and him alone. And this bride will never run after other lovers as King Solomon did. The Song of Songs unveils the beautiful imagery of love. The melody of the song along the journey weaves a picture of the two becoming one. The book portrays in living time the passionate desire between Christ and his church. It is also a picture representation of what God intends for marriage. It takes time to journey unto growth as there are highs and lows in the betrothal. The journey should eventually lead one to understand the length, the breadth, and the height of Christ's love for us along our journey.

The heartbeat of the Shulamite is found in chapter 1:4 in Song of Songs

Draw me, we will run after thee: the king hath brought me into his chambers: we will be glad and rejoice in thee, we will remember thy love more than wine: the upright love thee.

Oh! How I love that passage of scripture! It is one that influenced my life deeply and I pray often as I continue to see how badly I need him. The cry of the Shulamite was "Draw me." Her cry ignited a quest as well as gave the groom her consent and permission to come close. The definition of quest from the Oxford Language dictionary is a long arduous search for something. For me the key words are long and arduous. Once again not to be repetitive, it is a journey in our relationships. Anyone on a journey who stays the course will reach their destination. We will reach Christ as he draws us if we first give him permission. The scripture shows forth in Jeremiah 29:13. *"When we search and seek him with all our heart, we will find him."* I have listened to conversations and discussion from the Pharisees and Sadducees who think having a deep love relationship with God is over the top. They think such a relationship is extreme; it doesn't take all that. Well! My thought has been "Where do you think the ideal of marriage between and man and women came from? Where does the love and passion they have for one another come from?" Marriage, as in all things, is first spiritual and then physical. I will say it a hundred times and over. To the degree a person loves God will be to the degree they love their spouse. Period! That's a hill for me die on because God is LOVE and to know him is to love him. As we love him, we love others. Anything less than that, If we're not careful, we will find ourselves like King Solomon, with many others lovers who try to turn our hearts from God. Other lovers don't necessarily mean people. Let us awaken and renew our love and commitment to God along this journey. Trust me I have had to do it over and over again in my walk with God. I have to daily pray to keep other lovers and distractions out of my life. I must constantly ask his help to avoid anything that would steer me away from my course. So many times, along my journey, I have heard the still small voice of my father say "Stay the course." We have to keep our love burning and rekindle it as often as necessary. Remember, the Lord warned us in Revelation that the love of many had waxed cold. The book of Revelation is the last book of the Bible and we are in the last days. Let us heed that warning.

John 14:15 AMP reads

If you [really] love Me, you will keep and obey My commandments.

There is only one thing that will keep us from loving God and that is the S word - SIN. Sin separates and destroys. It puts a wedge between us and God in our relationship. Sin will hinder our pursuit for God. Let us hate sin and be adamant against it. I want to encourage you today in your journey. Remember, it only takes a spark to get a fire going. All the Shumate women was a small spark when she started her pursuit and quest for God, but she stuck to it. As she continued, her lover Christ began to draw her. Be encouraged! He will do the same for you and me.

To Know Me Is to Love Me

One morning while sitting in the presence of the Lord and simply enjoying him, praising him and loving him for who he is, he said "To know me is to love me. A stranger can never know me." I thought WOW! I had never quite looked at it from that perspective before, but it's true. I am a very inquisitive person when it comes to searching out scripture and its meaning. I decided to look up the word stranger in the dictionary. Stranger means a person whom one does not know or one is not familiar with. All I could say is wow! I have found myself saying many times "Lord, I love you." As I reflect back over my life, Christ was a stranger. I knew about him but I didn't really *know* him with an intimate relationship built on familiarity. To know Christ is to love him. God is love, and Christ is the embodiment of the love of God. Journey is so important because it allows us to come to really know Christ and to love him. I believe today is a good day for us to pause and reflect on our lives to make sure that we really love Christ. Do you really know him or is he a stranger? Are we still at the place in our walk and relationship with Christ that we were at when we first accepted him? Does his presence cause us to hunger and thirst for righteousness? Has he taken up residence in our hearts? Has his indwelling presence in us allowed our life to be conformed to his image? Are we striving to be Christ-like to some degree though not to full stature? Am I okay with just conversing with him on the run and not spending time with him, getting to know Him? I remember years ago I used to love a song titled "I Miss My Time With You." The song spoke of the Lord telling his people he missed spending time with them. He missed sharing moments together, moments that built relationship. He was saddened that his children now seemed too busy for him. Is that us today? If so, Christ has become a stranger to us. A stranger can never love God. Strangers are treated differently from someone we know. I mean, we teach our kids about stranger danger for their safety. Just as you or I would never marry a stranger, the Lord will never marry a bride who is a stranger to him.

To merely say "I Love you Lord" is empty and pointless. They are mere words until they are actually lived out in life expression, living expression. Just because I can talk about him, preach about him, write a book about him doesn't necessarily mean I know him. There is a difference. There's a difference in knowing him intimately and knowing *of* him. Words are only information until they become life. John 6:63 declares, *"My words are Spirit and they are life."* Once words become life, they have the power to change you. Your views, perceptions and perspectives are of our soul, our mind, will, and emotions. We have only mouth profession until there is heart possession. Life in Christ changes everything. As a seed looks small and insignificant, yet, once planted, it appears to achieve our desired results. It looks as though nothing could possibly change. However, life is in the seed and its appearance will change from the inside out. Christ does that in us as we are being conformed to his image and likeliness. As we grow in relationship and union with him our life will show a change.

When Christ looks into the beautiful eyes of his Bride she is known by him. He can see himself in her. She is known by him her groom; she is known because she is not a stranger. She has come to know him as she has journeyed with him in daily life. As she journeys with him through living circumstances she has become conformed in his image. Remember the Shulamite in Song of Songs? She said, "Now that I have found the one my soul loves I will not let him go." I believe when her journey started out, the one she loved was only a stranger to her. But through relationship, she was later able to say, "Now that I have found the one my soul loves." He was no longer a stranger to her as she had come to know him. I love the journey shown forth in the Song of Songs. In 2:14 he calls her his Dove and then in Song of Songs 4:2 he called her his Beloved! A name represents identity. They came to know one another along the journey called life. Christ is Life. Earlier in her journey in Song of Song 2:14 NKJV she asked to see his face. The scripture say as we behold him, we are being changed from glory to glory in his image, becoming one with him. (II Corinthians 3:18) She then asks, "Let me hear your voice." She wanted to know his voice so she would not follow or be misled by a stranger. She said his voice is sweet.

The scripture says in John 10:5

And a stranger will they not follow, but will flee from him: for they know not the voice of strangers.

As I said earlier, to know God is to love him. We must not only know about him but *know* him.

John 17:3

And this is life eternal, that they might know thee the only true God, and Jesus Christ, whom thou hast sent.

To know, perceive, recognize, become acquainted with, to understand. Growing in this type of relationship requires quality time being spent with Christ. Our beautiful Lord has many facets about him. There are many ways he speaks and reveals himself. He is like a rainbow with many beautiful colors, though it's only one rainbow. We must be able to recognize him that he may not become a stranger to us.

As I often say "Christ is a gentleman; he will knock before he comes in". He will never violate our freewill. It is by our desire that allows him to come close and draw us. The Apostle Paul said it was his determined purpose to know Christ in Philippians 3:10 AMP.

[For my determined purpose is] that I may know Him [that I may progressively become more deeply and intimately acquainted with Him,

perceiving and recognizing and understanding the wonders of His Person more strongly and more clearly], and that I may in that same way come to know the power outflowing from His resurrection [[a]which it exerts over believers], and that I may so share His sufferings as to be continually transformed [in spirit into His likeness even] to His death, [in the hope]

It was Paul's determined purpose to know Christ and progressively become more deeply and intimately acquainted with Christ. As I've said before, our journey is a progressive process. I love the fact that he said his determined purpose was to know Christ. His purpose was not to become something great or make a name for himself but to know Christ. As I have mentioned before Christ is a packaged deal. When you have him you have everything you need. All that he's meant for you will find you. We have no need to run for anything but Christ. Amen! And Amen!

Let us be mindful of Proverbs 8:17

I love those who love me, and those who seek me early and diligently shall find me.

Relationships are an investment, no deposit, no return. Those who love God and seek him will find him. Our deposit is seeking and time spent; our return will be we shall find him. May today be a new start to a new beginning of coming to know our Lord progressively. May we never allow him to be a stranger. We are his people, the sheep of his pasture, and we know his voice.(Psalm 100:3) Remember stranger danger. God bless.

The Barren Bride

While sitting at the table eating breakfast one beautiful morning in August while on vacation, I began to reflect on my life's journey and the many paths and directions the Lord has led me. I thought about some of my wishes, wants, desires over the many years. Sadly, it seemed that many of the things I had hoped to accomplish, I had yet to grasp. I pondered my hopes and was disappointed because what I thought my life would be in this decade of time was far from the reality I was experiencing. From my view and perspective some things looked in ruins. As I sat at the table the still small voice of the Lord spoke and said, "When you look at your life and say it doesn't seem like much has happened, remember this. The world was without form and I was yet creating. The world came into existence when it was without form, void and darkness crept upon the face of the earth. Your life may look like there is no form but I can yet create." He then sparked my memory of the barren women in the Bible. The barren women were empty, no form of life, no baby in her womb, but yet he said "I produced what she desired and could not bring forth."

I'm learning the beauty in the journey is that the creator removes the stress to perform from my life. He then reminds me that bringing something to pass is not on me or you. It's not meant for us to produce anything, build anything. All the producing of anything is Christ's business and not mine nor yours. In weakness our strength is made perfect so that Christ the perfect one will perfect all that concerns us.

My concern in the past has been, "Lord, how on earth can I make myself ready and become the beautiful bride you will marry? I am barren and have not the strength or the know-how." Here's the beautiful truth in the matter: Our beautiful helper the Holy Spirit will help us.

One day while studying I came across a scripture and one phrase jumped of the pages: **"When the time came."**

Galatians 4:4 NLT

But when the right time came, God sent his Son, born of a woman, subject to the law.

There was a right time for the barren women to conceive, and not before. From that passage of scripture, I now understand time is intertwined with the will of God. I have learned to quit worrying myself. I've stopped wondering why this and why that hasn't happened for me. As I sat at the breakfast table it was as though another peel of the onion of my darkened understanding was peeled back. The Lord said" Rochelle, the world was without form but I yet created." That was a Rema word for me, a word of life. I began to embark on a new journey of my life and I was starting to come out of a restless season. My motto is "If God doesn't do it, I can't!" And I found freedom in that. My prayer has become over and over. "Lord, come and do only what you can do." The word says "Be confident of this one thing, he that began a good work in you will perform it. (Philippians 1:6) I love the phrase 'Be confident.' I can tell you, that scripture has really helped me but also, it's something that I must remind myself of often. You know? Our self-life which is our mind, will, and emotions operates just like reflexes. If not brought under the control of the Holy Spirit, our self-life can cause knee-jerk reactions. Submission to the will of God isn't learned over night. Growth takes time. Growth and increase of Christ within us is a slow process of journeying with him daily. So be confident and breathe a little easier while leaning in on Christ, our perfector, and the Holy Spirit, our helper. In Zechariah 4:6 the word that came to Zerubbabel about his assignment laying the foundation of the Lord house. *"Not by power nor by might but by my Spirit says the Lord."*

I love it! There comes a point in our lives when our power in ourselves, our might to become this great suitable Bride for the Lord will be by his Spirit. Just like with Mary, the overwhelming wonderment of the fulfilling of the word of God and its process came by the power of the Lord. As the scripture goes on it says *"Who are you, great mountain?"* (Zechariah 4:7) That is shouting ground! Who are you? You great mountain of frustration, who are you? Great mountain of sickness? Who are you great mountain? These 'mountains' are nothing in comparison to the might and power of our Lord.

The Holy Spirit, our helper, our intercessor, our standby, stands by and if we allow him, he will do his job and be our great counselor and consultant in all matters of life. Let us become more aware of our helper, the one Christ left, his Holy Spirit. Let's allow the spirit to fulfill his role and function in our lives.

John 14:25-26 AMP

"I have told you these things while I am still with you. [d] Helper (Comforter, Advocate, Intercessor—Counselor, Strengthener, Standby), the Holy Spirit, whom the Father will send in My name[in My place, to represent Me and act on My behalf],He will teach you all things. And He will help you remember everything that I have told you.

It is imperative that we become acquainted with the Holy Spirit. All that he hears from the father he will speak. He plays a vital role in helping us to become the bride Christ desires to marry.

In Luke 1:25-31 the Angel Gabriel was sent by God to a town in Galilee called Nazareth, to the Virgin Mary engaged to Joseph of the house of David. The Angel came to Mary declaring Mary was blessed and highly favored among women; *"The Lord is with thee. Mary, behold thou shall conceive in the womb, and bring forth a son, and shall call his name JESUS."* (Luke 1:31)

When Mary encountered the angel, she was fearful and troubled. I am sure not only was she troubled but confused as to how this would happen. The angel said she would have a son, but she was not yet married. She knew the reproach such a thing would bring. She proceeded to ask the Angel in verse 34, *"How shall this be, seeing I know not man?"*

I love the response of the Angel. *"The Holy Ghost shall come upon thee, and the power of the Highest shall overshadow thee; therefore, also that holy thing which shall be born of thee, shall be called the Son of God."* (Luke 1:35) WOW! Putting myself in Mary's place I am sure I would still be confused due to the process and all the inner-workings to bring such a thing to pass. But as we read the continuation of the story, we see Mary walk though her journey and the word of the Lord was totally fulfilled in her life. One thing we know for sure. If not for the coming of Jesus, our Emanuel, none of us would be the same today. Can I get an Amen? If after the word declared by the Angel Gabriel from God wasn't fulfilled, salvation from sin would not have come to pass.

I also love the story of Manoah and his wife who was barren in the book of Judges chapter 13

And there was a certain man of Zorah, of the family of the Danites, whose name was Manoah; and his wife was barren, and bare not.

³And the angel of the Lord appeared unto the woman, and said unto her, Behold now, thou art barren, and bearest not: but thou shalt conceive, and bear a son.

⁴Now therefore beware, I pray thee, and drink not wine nor strong drink, and eat not any unclean thing:

⁵For, lo, thou shalt conceive, and bear a son; and no razor shall come on his head: for the child shall be a Nazarite unto God from the womb: and he shall begin to deliver Israel out of the hand of the Philistines.

We can see in Judges 13:24 that the Child Samson was born. We can clearly see that God has a purpose that was tied to time. When God's timing was right Manoah's wife conceived and was no longer barren. God's purpose for that birth was to deliver Israel, God's people, out of the hand of the Philistines. I am convinced there is beauty in barrenness. God is the only one that can bring forth birth and no self-will will ever be enough. When I think of a desert, I think of dry and barren. Not much can grow there except cactus. But grow they do – they bloom, grow and survive. Out of barrenness even nature blooms at the hand of the almighty God. Don't you just love it? He is so amazing and full of wonders.

Now let us look at this situation in our lives as we journey to know this Christ. I am certain God has not asked impossible things of you or me. He doesn't ask and then leave us. We can take a deep breath and know that through whatever we are facing today, God is with us, holding us by his mighty right hand. God will equip us for whatever he is requiring us to do. We can yield, follow him and allow him to work his plan. And he will!

If you noticed in the scripture, Mary too was on a journey to be married. Allegorically, Mary is a picture of the bride of Christ. She was espoused which means betrothed to Joseph. As I have said before, according to the Bible dictionary, betrothal means an act of engagement for marriage, in Bible times as binding as marriage itself. The Biblical terms betrothal and espousal are almost synonymous with marriage and as binding. In Jewish culture espoused is all about covenant, as it is with us. The covenant vow was made a year prior to the marriage and engagement was as binding as a marriage covenant. Consequently, a legal divorce was required to withdraw from the agreement. Wow! How serious! I can understand why marriage vows are not to be entered into lightly.

I'm sure you are wondering how significant this is in reference to our journey as a bride for Christ. All throughout the Bible Christ speaks much in reference to marriage and coming back for his bride. God's eternal purpose is to prepare a worthy bride and that takes time. In Matthew 22 the parable of the wedding banquet Christ sent forth his servants that were bidden to come. It's no different today. Just because someone proposes to you in marriage even with a shiny two carat engagement ring, it means nothing unless you agree to the engagement and say yes. The ring signifies a never-ending covenant but means nothing if you don't say YES. It's no different with us, Christ has bidden us to come to the marriage supper of the lamb, but we have a part to play. Our part is to say yes, and the preparations begin. Through consecrating ourselves to one lover Christ, laying our lives down and allowing him to make us ready though purification, we are drawn to his wedding feast table. (Revelation 14:13) The fine linen is the righteousness of saints; the righteous acts of the saints. That is, their former righteousness, exhibited in fidelity to God and hostility to the world, obtained and retained by the grace of God, now forms their chief glory. So "their works do follow them"

Testing and trials are a part of our maturing in the righteous acts as we experience Christ, but we must first say yes and accept his hand in marriage. Indeed, we do have a part to play. We say yes and allow him to make us ready. It is a journey day by day. How we live today matters.

Today my friends, I encourage you to take the next step in preparation to become the glorious bride. Remember it's a journey and make sure you take our friend the Holy Spirit and helper along.

Isaiah 54:1

"Sing, O childless woman, you who have never given birth! Break into loud and joyful song, O Jerusalem, you who have never been in labor. For the desolate woman now has more children than the woman who lives with her husband," says the LORD.

Time

Time is slippery; you can't catch it but you can keep track of it in reference to days, years, and seasons. Time is slipping through the hour glass of our lives. A. W. Tozer once said "When you kill time, remember that it has no resurrection." Wow! Couldn't have been said better. If only people knew how valuable it is in this hour, and how much it cost us in this day and time to live lives of holiness and preparation. Time is evasive, it's elusive and it waits for no man. Time is selfish; it stands alone. How important to know the times and season in which we live. To every season there is a time and purpose. Are you aware of the time you are living in and your purpose? Everything in creation speaks of time. For most there are four seasons in a year - Spring, Winter, Summer and Fall. Each season has a purpose and carries out its purpose; it has a time frame to come on the scene and to leave. We have a time we were born and a time to die. (Ecclesiastes 3:2) Within that frame of born-die there is a purpose for life and we have a certain amount of time to carry it out. Our first purpose is to know Christ and be conformed to his image and likeness. The Lord tells us to watch; when we see certain things happening in the world it would be an indication of the time and things to come.

Matthew 24:32

Now learn this lesson from the fig tree: As soon as its branches become tender and sprout leaves, you know that summer is near.

Have you ever heard the phrase, "Time is of the essence?" According the dictionary that phrase is said when there is something that must be done immediately. There is no time to waste, and whatever is being spoken about needs to be done fast. The meaning of time in the dictionary is 'A number, as of years, days, or minutes, representing such an interval.' Often the Lord continues to keep me alerted to the days and time we are living in. One thing I learned from Covid-19 (and I believe most of us did) is that so many people died suddenly and unexpectedly. More than likely most thought they had a lot of time to live. But that was not the case. I believe like I said before - I see going forward and learn looking backward. I understand the scripture and what it says in Hebrews 3:15. *"Today, if you hear his voice, do not harden your hearts as you did in the rebellion."* The key word is TODAY! For all we know today is all we really have. We know not the day nor the hour when we will draw our final breath. Today we are living in time. The trick is, time demands so much of us and has to be spread in so many different directions. Every day we must decide how we will spend our time. The Lord had me bring this subject to the forefront because it's easy for us to believe and be deceived that we always have tomorrow. That's just not the case.

The Bible speaks in II Timothy 3:1 of perilous times. *"But understand this, that in the last days will come (set in) perilous times of great stress and trouble [hard to deal with and hard to bear].*

Knowing this, we must use our time wisely and make sure Christ, who is the main thing, remains our focus. Anything that will steal our time from him will cause us to become careless. Carelessness always makes it easy to say, "I can do it tomorrow." Maybe so and maybe not. These are days that we need God's direction in our lives. I am reminded of the rich man who thought he had tomorrow.

Luke 12:16-18 AMP

16 Then He told them a parable, saying, The land of a rich man was fertile and yielded plentifully.

[17]And he considered and debated within himself, What shall I do? I have no place [in which] to gather together my harvest.

[18]And he said, I will do this: I will pull down my storehouses and build larger ones, and there I will store all[e] my grain or produce and my goods.

[19]And I will say to my soul, Soul, you have many good things laid up, [enough] for many years. Take your ease; eat, drink, and enjoy yourself merrily.

[20]But God said to him, You fool! This very night[f] they [the messengers of God] will demand your soul of you; and all the things that you have prepared, whose will they be?

The rich man took security and comfort in the fact that he had many goods stored up for MANY YEARS. He thought he could take his ease eating, drinking and being merry. But that night his soul was required of him. He thought he had tomorrow and made no preparation to meet the king. None. He found his life in riches. I'm sure it took lots of TIME to get rich but his time was not spent wisely. I hope we can see the importance of time and even more so in the days we are living. Out of all the things that demand our time, only the one thing, the main thing which is Christ, is worthy of dedicating our lives to. Christ is the one we need to spend our time on in order to be prepared to meet him. None of us know the day nor time we will leave this earth, but the important thing is that we are ready and prepared to meet him. (Matthew 25:13) Don't be caught off guard as the rich man was. I have a motto for myself: "Count each day, and make each day count." Time is expensive. We spend our time wisely when we spend time making sure our lives are balanced. We do have to live daily and do things that natural life requires. The balance of natural and spiritual is the key.

Peter is warning us in his epistle II Peter 3:8 AMP

Nevertheless, do not let this one fact escape you, beloved, that with the Lord one day is as a thousand years and a thousand years as one day.

Time means nothing to God because he is outside of time, but time means everything to us. Our perceptions of what time means to each of us individually will determine how we spend it, use it and make the most of. Delay is our perception, but God is long suffering not willing that any should perish. (II Peter 3:9) May we harken to the Apostle Peter and not let time escape us.

Sin ~ The Secret Assassin of the Bride

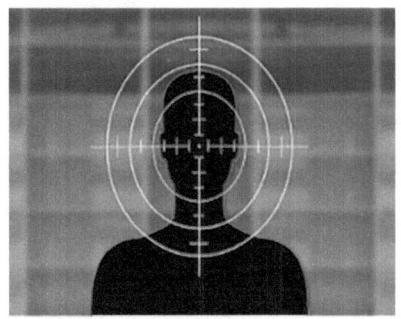

I'm reminded of a love story years ago in which a young girl fell in love with a man. After a prolonged relationship, she realized he was a criminal and narcissist. She knew he wasn't good for her but still loved him and was willing to overlook and accommodate for his antics. After all, she loved the way he made her feel, with his smooth words and gifts. She decided to stay with him and the longer she stayed, the more he began to control her life. Everything that was abnormal became normal for her. Even though she knew he was a criminal, she never once thought that the crimes he committed would inadvertently affect her life. All the inner alert systems she might have had were silenced by the false love, affection and attention the man was giving her. This story reminds me of sin and how it will operate in our lives if left unchecked.

Proverbs 9:17

Stolen waters are sweet, and bread eaten in secret is pleasant.

Sin offers momentary pleasure. Just like the story above, the girl wanted the pleasure of how the criminal made her feel. It was only for the moment though, because all sin is eventually judged. Sin traps us as it did the lady because it is sweet. It tastes good and feels good but eventually, if not careful, the love of sin has deadly effects and can continually draw a person into their own lust which can lead to becoming an addict.

Proverbs 20:17

Food gained by deceit is sweet to a man, but afterward his mouth will be filled with gravel [just as sin may be sweet at first, but later its consequences bring despair.]

Sin has carnal sensual pleasures. It is a false pleasure because it wasn't given by God. In the end it leads to disappointment. The Bible says sin is only for a season because it steals, kills and destroys. I remember hearing someone say "Sin is like signing your name to a blank check because you don't know what the price will be." Could not have been said better! That's why I view sin as a secret assassin, hired by Satan.

The dictionary defines an assassin as a person who kills, someone hired to kill. I am not sure if you ever thought of sin like that but in all actuality, the effects of sin are usually, though not always, seen immediately. The ramifications do come from the hit man.

Ecclesiastes 8:11-13

¹¹ Because sentence against an evil work is not executed speedily, therefore the heart of the sons of men is fully set in them to do evil.

¹² Though a sinner do evil an hundred times, and his days be prolonged, yet surely I know that it shall be well with them that fear god, which fear before him.

¹³ But it shall not be well with the wicked, neither shall he prolong his days, which are as a shadow, because he feared not before God. Those who fear God will fear sin.

II Corinthians 2:11

We cannot afford to be ignorant lest Satan should get an advantage over us.

What I am witnessing and have for quite some time in the lives of believers is this: sin has become tolerable in Christiandom and accepted under the guise of "No one is perfect," or "Don't judge." Yet the word clearly speaks of a righteous judgment. (John 7:24) The reality is, sin kills. Period. And until the sin nature of Adam is dealt with in each of us, we will continue to willfully sin with the excuse of "I'm not perfect." Some may ask, how is the sin nature dealt with? The answer is found at the foot of the Cross of Christ. Here we lay down our wills and the two intersect Many people sit in a church, go to a church for years, and equate going to church with being saved and having a personal relationship with the Lord. However, nothing can be further from the truth. The word says the devil believes and trembles. (James 2:19) He also goes to church! Lucifer was kicked out of heaven because of his pride. Lucifer boldly declared in Isaiah 14:12-15

[12] How are thou fallen from heaven, O Lucifer, son of the morning! How are thou cut down to the ground, which didst weaken the nations!

[13] For thou hast said in thine heart, I will ascend into heaven, I will exalt my throne about the stars of God. I will sit also upon the count of the congregation, in the sides of the north:

[14] I will ascend above the heights of the clouds; I will be like the most High.

[15] Yet thou shalt be brought down to hell, to the sides of the pit.

I sure see a lot of 'I will's!' This I is all about flesh, the mind, will and emotions. Clearly we need not make a mistake and can clearly see that flesh kills and destroys us. Anything that is not of the Spirit is of the flesh. The one thing I find amazing is that pride was the number one sin. Pride got Lucifer kicked out of heaven. I mean, there was not like a list of sins that got him kicked out. Moses was shut out of the Promised Land for the one sin of striking the rock. I believe there is much we can gain from that to keep away from the pit-fall of the assassin. You may ask what I mean. Well, it does not take a whole list of sins to get us into hell. It only takes one unrepented sin. Let us be watchful of the assassin, the hit man who can take us down with one shot. That alone should awaken us.

God gave his only son Jesus Christ because of our sins, so that we might have eternal life. So, I ask today, "What are we giving Christ?" It should be our lives laid down. If not, may we come to understand that the price Christ paid for us was a great price. One day while studying the word, the Lord said, "When people come to understand the HIGH price I paid, they will stop living CHEAP lives.

What is cheap living? It is a selfish life which is self-centered. A life that caters to what it wants, feels and thinks, instead of being a yielded vessel. A yielded vessel will deny itself and take up the cross, following Christ daily at all cost. Sin must not be allowed to reign in our bodies. Sin is what causes spots and blemishes on our bridal gown.

Matthew 16:24-26 AMP

24Then Jesus said to His disciples, "If anyone wishes to follow me [as my disciple]. He must deny himself [set aside selfish interests],and take up his cross [expressing a willingness to endure whatever may come] and follow Me [believing in Me, conforming to My example in living and, if need be, suffering or perhaps dying because of faith in Me].

25For whoever wishes to save his life [in this world] will [eventually] lose it [through death], but whoever loses his life [in this world] for My sake will find it [that is, life with Me for all eternity.]

26For what will it profit a man if he gains the whole world [wealth, fame success] but forfeits his soul? Or what will a man give in exchange for his soul?"

Matthew makes it very clear to us in his gospel. If we desire to be Christ's disciple, we must deny ourselves, lose sight of and forget our own interests. There are no options if we wish to be his disciple. From this portion of scripture, we can agree that it will cost us something to follow Christ. It costs more than casually going to church without relationship. It costs more that just being comfortable with only religion.

Webster defines religion as a personal set of institutionalized system of religious attitude, beliefs and practices. There are no options if we wish to be his disciple. If we are not careful, religion opens the door to the way of ease as described in Amos 6:1. When it comes to the assassin sin, we must not let ease become seated in our lives so much so that we make light of sin when we are confronted by it in our lives. We must not allow its solicitations to draw us in by way of our senses and fleshly desires. We must stand up, fight, and resist. Ease is always easy because it appeases our flesh and wants what it wants, when it wants it. It will always offer the easy way out at the time, but it is costly. Trust me; the assassin is always on the hunt looking for its next victim. We must have a deep personal relationship with Christ if we are to overcome. It is a fight that strengthens through our relationship with Christ. Mere self-control alone will not be strong enough. Christ and the arising of his life in and through us by way of relationship will conquer our enemies. The Pharisees and Sadducees are great examples of those who practiced religion without relationship. It's like they had community without communion and relationship. They were known amongst their community but religion kept them from a true relationship with Christ. They were fault finders – never seeing the good, never forming true relationship with Christ as he walked the earth. They were completely bent on law, rules and regulations. That was their focus, much more than a relationship with Christ, who at the time was walking as a teacher among them. They were doing all the outward things, keeping the rules, celebrating the feast in the temple daily, yet without relationship with Christ. A deep personal relationship with Christ is the Kryptonite that will defeat the assassin sin.

We are living in such perilous times. These days are a solemn warning. We need to be sober-minded and serious about what is happening around us. At some point we must awaken to the darkness and wonder how it got to be this bad. I can tell you, the assassin sin came in through the open doors of our nations, lives, families and church. Sin has run rampant so therefore God must sound the trumpet to awaken his true church. The Bible says we are the light of the world, (Matthew 5:14) but unfortunately, darkness is creeping in. Changes must be made in all of our lives and we all must decide if we want to be on the Lord's side and not the side of religion, our church, and doing our own thing. God will never marry a bride that is not totally, wholeheartedly his. Christ is looking for an instrument that he can use to conquer and overcome the darkness that has set in. Like I have said, there's a price to be paid. Either the price will be one we are willing to pay or we will go our separate way, apart from Christ. We must lay down our lives if we are to go with God.

Starting out, for me it was so easy to be in fellowship with other believers, singing and praising God in his presence. I was filled with love and it was easy to say "I love you Lord." But as soon as I left that atmosphere, my love for God immediately became challenged. The Lord began to teach me in scripture what it really means to love him.

1 John 2:15-17AMP

15Do not love the world [of sin that opposes God and his precepts]. Nor the things that are in the world. If anyone loves the world, the love of the Father is not in him.

16For all that is in the world, the lust and sensual craving of the flesh and the lust and longing of the eyes and the boastful pride of life [pretentious confidence in one's resources or in the stability of earthly things' – these do not come from the father, but are from the world.

17The world is passing away, and with it its lusts [the shameful pursuits and ungodly longings]; but the one who does the will of God and carries out His purposes lives forever.

Through this passage I came into greater clarity and understanding of what it means to love God. It went beyond mere words and religious acts and duties. It brought me onto the ground of humility and commitment. It brought me to the foot of the cross. I understand that the price of sin is a blank check. Believers, loving God is a forever lifestyle and nothing we could ever offer God other than ourselves will matter. God is not and will not ever be impressed with our good works. Good works will not save us. (Ephesians 2:9) It doesn't matter to him how well we can sing, how many books we can write, or how well we can teach. Nothing like that matters to him. What he wants is ALL OF US! And giving ourselves to him is a choice that we must make. We must decide to live for him. We must defeat the assassin.

I challenge us today to let go of our own homemade plans and desires for our lives and allow Christ to become Lord over everything. When we deny ourselves, we gain, and what we hold on to we lose.

We all have a daily cross to carry - the laying down of our lives. Yes, it will cost us some troubles, pain and suffering because the word says in Galatians 5:17 *"For the flesh lusteth against the Spirit, and the Spirit against the flesh: and these are contrary the one to the other: so that ye cannot do the things that ye would."* It was not easy for Christ either, but he didn't come down from the Cross which is what the enemy wanted him to do and us as well. I pray today that God will make us his people so sin-sick that we will beg for mercy and come into the reality of the assassin. Either we take him out or he will take us out. We will decide.

So, my question to us today is: Will we come down from the Cross when our feelings and emotions are screaming at us to go ahead and do what we want, or will we too stay on the Cross? Will we stay on the cross when all our friends are going the opposite direction instead of the narrow way? Be aware! The assassin is never far away. Always remember that sin will at first fascinate you but then it will assassinate you. Selah!

Alabaster Box the Expensive Lifestyle of the Bride

I remember in my younger days my friends and I loved watching the soap operas. We made sure we never missed an episode. Every episode was filled with drama, betrayal, and so much more. One particular episode that stood out is one when two lovers were to be married and her groom was rich. The stipulation for her marriage was that she must sign a prenuptial agreement. I am not clear on all the ins and outs of prenups so I took it upon myself to do a little research. I looked for information about prenup agreements on Wikipedia. A prenuptial agreement, antenuptial agreement, or premarital agreement(commonly referred to as a prenup) is a written contract entered into by a couple before marriage or a civil union that enables them to select and control many of the legal rights they acquire upon marrying, and what happens when their marriage eventually ends by death or divorce. In recent years the number of prenups has skyrocketed. I think, in many ways, that is sad because love isn't or should never be based on the ownership or acquisition of things. At least it is not what God would base marriage on, and should not be so with Christians. God is love. Is it really love when people marry based on stipulations and not the total giving of one's self?

How many know God is an all or nothing God? He will never accept half of us or any stipulations other than to love him with our whole heart. He loves us and is covenanted with us based on love. Period. I have found as I have journeyed with God, though I started out not giving myself fully to him, overtime as our relationship began to grow and he drew me to himself, I began to give all and relinquished more and more of myself to him. I began to loosen my grip on the things that I wanted to control early on in our relationship. The more I came to know him, the more I loved him and all I wanted to do was please him and give him all of me. My love for him was not based on what I could get or what he could give me. Yes, my alabaster box with all my precious perfumes of my heart's desires, my best wishes of what I wanted to be and become, was all poured out at his feet. My alabaster box became filled with my love for him and I poured it all out in the total and complete giving of myself. The pouring of my oil was symbolism of my becoming nothing that he could become everything to me, in me, and through me. Yes, it's a journey of daily pouring out all of me.

Over the years, I have been so drawn to the woman with the alabaster jar in Matthew 26:7-12 NLT

> [7] *While he was eating,*[b] *a woman came in with a beautiful alabaster jar of expensive perfume and poured it over his head.*

> [8] *The disciples were indignant when they saw this. "What a waste!" they said.* [9] *"It could have been sold for a high price and the money given to the poor."*

> [10] *But Jesus, aware of this, replied, "Why criticize this woman for doing such a good thing to me?* [11] *You will always have the poor among you, but you will not always have me.* [12] *She has poured this perfume on me to prepare my body for burial.* [13] *I tell you the truth, wherever the Good News is preached throughout the world, this woman's deed will be remembered and discussed."*

The women poured out the expensive oil on Jesus. I believe it was her life savings, and represented her life and love for the master and who he was. From the scripture it appears she understood who Jesus was even more than the disciples did. They thought it was a waste for her to pour it out on Jesus. Isn't it interesting that the disciples had been with Jesus for several years but still didn't really know him for who he was? That day the disciples were the onlookers; they were outside looking in and made their judgment based on the external. Oh! But Jesus based his from the inside out. He saw and knew what was in the woman's heart. He said in verse 13 that what she had done would be preached through the world and her deeds would be remembered and discussed. So it is today. Onlookers are those that seem to be the ones to say. "It don't take all that to serve God." They are the ones that have an opinion on how and why you serve God. They are critical of the way you worship and question your passion for him. Why? Because they don't know the price of your oil. They don't understand the cost you have paid to have the total and complete will of God fulfilled in your life. The word says in

Matthew 16:24

Then Jesus said to His disciples, "If anyone wishes to follow Me[as My disciple],he must deny himself[set aside selfish interests],and take up his cross[expressing a willingness to endure whatever may come]and follow Me[believing in Me, conforming to My example in living and, if need be, suffering or perhaps dying because of faith in Me].

We can see from this portion of scripture that it's costly to follow Christ and become his disciple. I'm also reminded of the story in Luke 7:36-38 NLT

37When a certain immoral woman from that city heard he was eating there, she brought a beautiful alabaster jar filled with expensive perfume.

38Then she knelt behind him at his feet, weeping. Her tears fell on his feet, and she wiped them off with her hair. Then she kept kissing his feet and putting perfume on them.

³⁹When the Pharisee who had invited him saw this, he said to himself, "If this man were a prophet, he would know what kind of woman is touching him. She's a sinner!"

⁴⁰Then Jesus answered his thoughts. "Simon," he said to the Pharisee, "I have something to say to you."

"Go ahead, Teacher," Simon replied.

⁴¹Then Jesus told him this story: "A man loaned money to two people—500 pieces of silver[i] to one and 50 pieces to the other. ⁴²But neither of them could repay him, so he kindly forgave them both, canceling their debts. Who do you suppose loved him more after that?"

⁴³Simon answered, "I suppose the one for whom he canceled the larger debt."

"That's right," Jesus said. ⁴⁴Then he turned to the woman and said to Simon, "Look at this woman kneeling here. When I entered your home, you didn't offer me water to wash the dust from my feet, but she has washed them with her tears and wiped them with her hair. ⁴⁵You didn't greet me with a kiss, but from the time I first came in, she has not stopped kissing my feet. ⁴⁶You neglected the courtesy of olive oil to anoint my head, but she has anointed my feet with rare perfume.

⁴⁷"I tell you, her sins—and they are many—have been forgiven, so she has shown me much love. But a person who is forgiven little shows only little love." ⁴⁸Then Jesus said to the woman, "Your sins are forgiven."

⁴⁹The men at the table said among themselves, "Who is this man, that he goes around forgiving sins?"

⁵⁰And Jesus said to the woman, "Your faith has saved you; go in peace."

My God! I just love this parable. A woman, an immoral woman, a sinner, came in and poured out her expensive oil on Jesus, wiped his feet with her tears, and dried them with her hair. Oh yes! An immoral woman came in the face of her accusers, the Pharisees. She was a woman that knew who she was but more than that knew WHO JESUS WAS. She understood even more than the disciples who walked with him daily. She gave all she had, poured it out. Jesus had to break it down to the disciples. He said she had been forgiven much because her sins were many and she showed much love. He went on to say a person who is forgiven little shows only little love. WOW! Could that be why it's hard for some to pour it all out on Jesus? Because they are not aware of how bad off they are and how badly they need him? Therefore, their thoughts are as the disciples, that the oil was wasted and could have been sold. Regardless of what we say with our mouths, and how much we say we love God, it comes down to how we live and how we GIVE ourselves to the Lord. Where and how we pour our oil is and will always be a reflection of our relationship with God. Our actions speak louder than words. God is an all or nothing God. Lord, may we not be as the disciples, simply onlookers and unaware of who you really are. We all are pouring our love out somewhere. My prayer is that we pour it on Jesus and nothing and no one else.

I so love this story because it is my story. I was once the immoral women who was broken and without hope. Oh! I'm so thankful for the day when Jesus saved my soul. Now I'm giving back ALL the praise, ALL of my love and ALL of me. I will forever pour my oil because as the song says "You don't know the cost of the oil in my praise nor my Alabaster Box." Because I have been forgiven MUCH I LOVE much. I am humbled by the love of God and grateful. My song to God has become "I in you and you in me" and ain't nothing nobody can do about it! I've been forgiven. One thing I do know, no one will ever receive God's fullness when they hold back part of themselves.

Oh! I can't leave out the the widow of Zarephath in I Kings 17:8-12

8 Then the Lord said to Elijah,9 "Go and live in the village of Zarephath, near the city of Sidon. I have instructed a widow there to feed you."

10 So he went to Zarephath. As he arrived at the gates of the village, he saw a widow gathering sticks, and he asked her, "Would you please bring me a little water in a cup?"¹¹As she was going to get it, he called to her, "Bring me a bite of bread, too."

¹²But she said, "I swear by the Lord your God that I don't have a single piece of bread in the house. And I have only a handful of flour left in the jar and a little cooking oil in the bottom of the jug. I was just gathering a few sticks to cook this last meal, and then my son and I will die."

¹³But Elijah said to her, "Don't be afraid! Go ahead and do just what you've said, but make a little bread for me first. Then use what's left to prepare a meal for yourself and your son. ¹⁴For this is what the Lord, the God of Israel, says: There will always be flour and olive oil left in your containers until the time when the Lord sends rain and the crops grow again!"

¹⁵So she did as Elijah said, and she and Elijah and her family continued to eat for many days. ¹⁶There was always enough flour and olive oil left in the containers, just as the Lord had promised through Elijah.

If you and I have been forgiven much, we will love much. Is your alabaster box costly and ready to be poured out?

You Have Captured My Heart

I love the song lyrics "You have captured my heart, now I am yours, completely yours." Oh! How those lyrics resonate within me. No one ever thinks of being captured as a good thing because its meaning can suggest being forced or taken against one's will. Oh! But when it comes to God, nothing can be further from the truth. With Christ to be captured by him is to be taken by surprise, overwhelmed by his goodness and who he is.

I'm sure we can all relate to going out on date for the first time. You receive counsel from your friends giving advice as to if you should go or not go with the person. All the do's and dont's are based on what your friends might know or not know of the person. Truth be told, you made your own decision, even when you went against the opinion of others. When you went out you found things were not as others had said or thought. Even though perhaps, the person didn't quite meet your list of preferences, there was something about them that drew you in. Before you knew it, over time you discovered that this was the person for you. They had captured your heart with their kindness, gentleness and respect. You had been captured.

When I think about being captured can't help but think again about the Shulamite women in Song of Songs. Talk about being captured! The Shulamite women's journey began with her seeking and engaging the king. She ended up being captured by him. Her heart became captured and she became his. I'm not quite sure of the mind of the daughters of Jerusalem though. They said in Song of Songs chapter 1 *"We will run after you, we will remember your love more than wine"*. From the scripture Song of Songs 2:2 the King compared his Bride to a lily among thorns, meaning the other women were not worth noticing in comparison to the Shulamite. Her heart became settled in him. She said, "Now that I have found the one my soul loves I will not let him go." Obviously, an awakening had taken place within her. There was a pursuit that led to the capturing of her heart. In Song of Songs 1:5 she declares *"Your love is better than wine."* God is love and his love covers everything, even a multitude of sin. God's love offered her everything that her emotions could not offer or manipulate. Because God is love, he never changes; he is always consistent in his nature.

She became captured by his love and followed his tracks as she inquired of his whereabouts. I love the song and the picture it portrays. It leaves tracks for us and hints about how to follow Christ and pursue him.

The word says in Jeremiah 29:13 AMP

Then [with a deep longing] you will seek Me and require Me [as a vital necessity] and [you will] find Me when you search for Me with all your heart.

We find him if we want to find him. We must come to see he is our vital necessity, as did the Shulamite women. She said *"Now that I have found the one my soul loves I will not let him go."* (Song of Songs 3:4.) May we see the Lord is calling us unto himself in a deeper, more personal, intimate relationship. However, as you read and study the story, they never pursued the King as the Shulamite. As I have previously said there are many virgins but only one bride. The Shulamite pursued engagement; she caused him to become interested or involved. This engagement first came before the other type of engagement, which is betrothal the period of time between a marriage proposal and the actual marriage as quoted in Webster. In the engagement process you capture the heart of the king. It will be not different for us.

I am not sure who all will read this book and what level of relationship you are on, if at all. For those who are interested with starting or are continuing on the journey of relationship with your Lord, follow this path as the Shulamite and allow Christ to draw you. Engage him by way of humility and prayer. He will hear and answer you. One thing I know for sure, in the days ahead without a serious and faithful relationship with the Lord, we're in trouble. It will be to our determent to not have a deep relationship and trust in the Lord. We will face things that will require our love for Christ to arise above everything. Only for love will one lay down his life for his friend. I have found on my journey, my words, though many times spoken in full passion and commitment, fell short because I realized I could not trust Christ any further than what I knew him. Though I knew him and believed him to be the God that can work miracles and do anything, I still didn't know him personally. It was hard to believe he could or would do anything for me. Intimate relationship and fellowship unto commitment is necessary. We have our part to play. It first starts with engagement which allows God to encounter us. God is love and it is him who is love that creates and teaches us how to love him. So take a breath, allow him to do it through us. The Shulamite came to realize to that it was his love that covered her as she said "Your banner over me is love." (Song of Songs 2:4) Love, God's love in our lives, covers everything. He is our banner and shield, but just knowing this is not enough. We must experience him to be love in our lives as he draws us. In love there is trust, and we come to trust him in our lives and relationship with him. We begin to relinquish our precious things such as secret hurts, hidden desires, unholy thoughts, and things we try to control. I urge you to unleash them in his hands today. Let him draw you into a deep relationship of love.

Song of Song 2:7 AMP

I command that you take an oath, O daughters of Jerusalem,
By the gazelles or by the doe's of the field [which run free],
That you do not rouse nor awaken my love
Until she pleases."

She had found her love; it found its resting place in her heart. She wanted nothing to touch or distract it. From that point everything changed. He said, "Come with me, my beautiful one." (Song of Songs 2:10) He could not invite her any farther in their relationship until she had experienced love and knew how much he loved her. It's no different for us. Until we accept and come to know how much Christ loves us, our relationships will be stagnant. Stagnation will hinder the different levels of our love we can experience. The word speaks of the length the dept the breadth and height of his love.

Ephesians 3:18-19 NLT

And may you have the power to understand, as all God's people should, how wide, how long, how high, and how deep his love is.[19] May you experience the love of Christ, though it is too great to understand fully. Then you will be made complete with all the fullness of life and power that comes from God.

Look how beautiful this scripture is, friends. I really want to live this scripture out. I desire a deeper understanding of God's love; I want and desire to experience it in fullness. He says his love makes us complete. My God! When we are complete in God's love, we never have to compete with anyone or anything. We never have to seek the approval of man. I am sure that is a battle we all have fought or maybe we are currently fighting. It takes something to walk alone when you are going after God to know him deeper. Your life does not look like everybody else. People formed their opinions from the outside looking in. Oh well! God's love makes us complete. I have found a deeper love and have encountered real love along my journey. As the Shulamite, it has caused my mind to be turned and my heart in tuned more toward him. As I began to search more for him, the more he revealed and reveals himself. Once the Shulamite found love even on her night bed her thoughts of her lover remained. (Song of Songs 3:1.)

When I began to really get out to God and I began to study this book over and over again to understand it and experience God, I began to see how much Christ desired a relationship with me. The Lord let me know that many people think this type of relationship just can't happen or is over the top. But he told me, "I created marriage and relationship. I created man to fellowship with God and to know him intimately and personally. Enoch figured that out which is why I took him." God began to tell me to look at different examples in the world to make a comparison. He said, "Look, people have relationships with sports; coaches have relationships with their players. Sport teams take pride on relationship building and connection with one another." It's been said the more the players know one another and bonds with each other strengthen, they will play better. Friends create relationships and bond by spending time together. Anything we give our time and attention to, we create some type of attachment or bonding with.

People who are a part of organization, club, team or everything else will even pay dues to be members. So why does a deep personal relationship with God seem so odd to some? The book of Song of Songs seems over the head for some. There is no greater relationship one can have than with Christ who is the relationship creator. In closing I want to quote Song of Song 8:14 AMP

"Hurry, my beloved and come quickly, like a gazelle or a young stag [taking me home] On the mountains of spices."

Friends, it's time we make haste and get out to the Lord. It's time for deeper intimate relationships to be established as we see the day approaching. Remember we only pass this way once. When we leave this earth, we cannot return and make changes to our regrets. We only have one chance to become the bride and that's now. Tomorrow might be too late. Yes, there is the church which is in some ways in similarity to the daughters of Jerusalem as I mention. But there was only one Bride. May we choose wisely.

I will never forget one day in prayer the Lord made something so plain to me. He said, "Rochelle, the day I return, which some reference as the rapture of the church, is a big wedding day. So if people do not want to spend time with me while here on earth, why would they want to go to heaven? Because I am heaven, and you will find me there." I may have mentioned this in a previous journal but it bears weight in repeating again. Wow! AWAKEN!

If you have never established a deep personal relationship with Christ, why not let today be the day? Awaken Oh Bride! Awaken unto the love of Christ.

Eternal Flame

One morning while rising I turned my heart to the father in a time of prayer. I began to pray without thought. "Lord, I pray may your eternal flame, the eternal flame you are, forever burn in me and never go out." This was not a planned prayer in reference to what I was praying previously but came completely out of my spirit. As the day moved on, I pondered what the Lord was speaking to me. I began to study in his word and search out the scriptures. As I have said before *"It's the glory of the Lord to reveal a matter but the honor of Kings to search it out."* (Proverbs 25:2) I have found along my journey many times this is the way the Lord will lead as he did the Shulamite women. It was along the paths where he fed his flock. He will also feed us if we choose to seek, enquire, and follow in his footsteps.

When I began to think of the eternal flame my mind was drawn back to the ones you see sometimes at different burials as a memorial. Webster defines eternal flame is a small fire that is kept burning as a symbol to show that something will never end. All I can say is wow - something that will never end! As I continue to move to the close of this book, I pray that we have gained some insight into the heart and mind of Christ and found him in a new light. I see why the Lord referred to the eternal flame because it must never be allowed to go out in our lives. The flame of our relationship with the father must never be extinguished. God is eternal and offers us eternal life. Eternity is infinite in duration. Our abiding fellowship with Christ should be no less. Hebrews 12:29 tells us God is a consuming fire. When I embrace the fact that God is love, his love is consuming. It overtakes our lives if we allow it. If not, then something or someone else consumes us and extinguishes our love for him. At the same time God is also a jealous God and will consume anything that threatens his true bride. Notice the key word is *true* bride. I used to always hear the old church mothers talk about fire on the altar, which is prayer and sacrifice. A sacrifice is our lives being continually laid down. Continually, eternally laid down on the altar to be totally consumed by God. We must be careful because I am seeing a lot of smoke but no fire. II Timothy 2:5 says *"Having a form of godliness, but denying the power thereof: from such turn away."* Wow! Doing all the right things outwardly but with an inward heart that does not fully belong to God is like putting up a smoke screen. If you hear nothing else I ever say in this book remember this please. God never leaves a man or women the way he found them. If our lives are the same as the day we were saved then something is wrong. Christ in us is Christ through us. I have to sound the trumpet hard and hit this by the Spirit of God. Christ in US is Christ THROUGH US! Period. A change takes place. A half-hearted form of godliness extinguishes the eternal flame. It's all or nothing. Believe me, when Christ comes in us, he will NEVER allow us to live the same way before we accepted him. I am appalled when I hear people who say they are Christians, cussing, drinking, smoking, watching filthy movies, living in adultery and the likes thereof. Oh, this is not to be critical but awakening. The Lord is trying to reach people as time draws nigh. Eternal damnation is just as real as eternal life. May we awaken? I see Christ in his word rebuking and chastening those that he loves. (See Hebrews 12:6)

When King Solomon built the temple in the Holy Place there were ten golden lamps which had to be trimmed regularly by the Priest of the temple to ensure they were never extinguished. My God! Never extinguished, never to go out. That was in the natural realm of tradition at that time. Now how much more for us who are the living sanctuary of Christ! In Psalms 18: 28 we read

For You cause my lamp to be lighted and to shine; The LORD my God illumines my darkness.

Christ within is the eternal light within. We choose to allow him to shine bright or we dim our light through sin. All sin does is slowly put a damper in our light and over time it will be extinguished completely. A great example is the Priest Eli you can reference in I Samuel chapter 3. Overtime Eli became a Priest who would not judge his sons for the sins they were committing in the temple. That in itself was sin. The scripture references that his eyes began to wax dim, that he could not see. This blinding was a natural representation of what had happened to him spiritually. Overtime his light had dimmed and eventually diminished. Because of this the Lord judged and removed him. Let that not be us, my friends. Let us allow Christ in our life to shine brightly through us.

Proverbs 20:27

The spirit of man is the candle of the Lord, searching all the inward parts of the belly.

This scripture clearly stated WE are the candle of the Lord. His eternal flame is within us.

Psalms 119:105 reads

Thy word is a lamp unto my feet, and a light unto my path.

How great his word is! We have a lamp that will guide us along our daily journey of life.

As I said from the start of this journal, Christ is a flame that is meant to be kept burning and never extinguished. We find in the word of God an example where the flame was totally extinguished.

Matthew 25:13

Then shall the kingdom of heaven be likened unto ten virgins, which took their lamps, and went forth to meet the bridegroom.

²And five of them were wise, and five were foolish.

³They that were foolish took their lamps, and took no oil with them:

⁴But the wise took oil in their vessels with their lamps.

⁵While the bridegroom tarried, they all slumbered and slept.

⁶And at midnight there was a cry made, Behold, the bridegroom cometh; go ye out to meet him.

⁷Then all those virgins arose, and trimmed their lamps.

⁸And the foolish said unto the wise, give us of your oil; for our lamps are gone out.

⁹But the wise answered, saying, Not so; lest there be not enough for us and you: but go ye rather to them that sell, and buy for yourselves.

¹⁰And while they went to buy, the bridegroom came; and they that were ready went in with him to the marriage: and the door was shut.

¹¹Afterward came also the other virgins, saying, Lord, Lord, open to us.

¹²But he answered and said, Verily I say unto you, I know you not.

¹³Watch therefore, for ye know neither the day nor the hour wherein the Son of man cometh.

All I can say is My God! What a profound warning! The foolish virgins were not prepared as they let their lamps, their eternal flame, go completely out. Lord, help us. As I pondered on this parable I thought, it had to have been totally dark when they went back to buy oil, naturally speaking. The journey had to be difficult. Without the flame they were not able to see at all. And the most devastating thing of all to me is it seems they would have made it back still in good standing with the bride groom because they now had bought oil and returned. But to their determent, the door was tightly shut. May our eyes be opened today so that we see the importance of preparation. The eternal flame that Christ is within us we must NEVER ALLOW TO BE DIMINISHED AND GO COMPLETELY OUT. May we all choose to stay filled with God, consumed with him. Today the Lord is blasting the trumpet; let those that have ears to hear heed the warning. Hear the word of the Lord today. Awaken Oh Bride! Stay eternally ablaze for God. It only takes a spark to get a fire started. The hour is late.

Looking Unto Jesus

Looking Unto Jesus is a word of finality as we reach the end of our journey in reference to the reading of this book. I can't help to look unto Jesus to be encouraged and gain the strength to continue to journey when I see so much depravity in our nation and world. I mean I have read and pondered the story of Sodom and Gomorrah many times. My heart faints when I see so much resemblance to Sodom and Gomorrah in our nation. Some days I feel like a child peeking through the covers because you are not sure what you will see or find lurking in the darkness of the room. *"Even as Sodom and Gomorrah, and the cities about them in like manner, giving themselves over to fornication, and going after strange flesh, are set forth for an example, suffering the vengeance of eternal fire."* (Jude 1:7)

I believe if we are all honest with ourselves, we can see the resemblance to Sodom and Gomorrah in the United of America. Oh America, sadly your crown has fallen from your head. Ecclesiastes1:9 NLT declares *"The thing that hath been, it is that which shall be; and that which is done is that which shall be done: and there is no new thing under the sun."*

From this passage of scripture God is not taken by surprise at the evil and neither should we because nothing is new under the sun. Therefore, we look unto Jesus. We have a cloud of witnesses that have gone on before us and have come through times such as these. One may ask well! What must we do? We can find our answer in Hebrews 12:1-4 NLT

Therefore, since we are surrounded by such a huge crowd of witnesses to the life of faith, let us strip off every weight that slows us down, especially the sin that so easily trips us up. And let us run with endurance the race God has set before us.² We do this by keeping our eyes on Jesus, the champion who initiates and perfects our faith.[a] Because of the joy[b] awaiting him, he endured the cross, disregarding its shame. Now he is seated in the place of honor beside God's throne.³ Think of all the hostility he endured from sinful people;[c] then you won't become weary and give up.⁴ After all, you have not yet given your lives in your struggle against sin.

We must lay aside every weight and the sin which easily besets us and run the race. We run the race by looking unto Jesus. Yes, we see all the evil and depravity around us but we keep our focus, our eyes on Jesus. We must not let the weight of sin tip the scales of our lives unto selfish living which leads to eternal damnation. As we look unto Jesus there is a joy that is set before us because of what is to come, what awaits us, and what is to come in him. There is a joy to beholding Christ as the one we wait for. As we continue to journey through these dark turbulent times, we must already be prepared from the onset. Just as Jesus endured the cross, so must we.

Matthew 16:24 AMP

Then Jesus said to His disciples, "If anyone wishes to follow Me [as My disciple], he must deny himself [set aside selfish interests], and take up his cross [expressing a willingness to endure whatever may come] and follow Me [believing in Me, conforming to My example in living and, if need be, suffering or perhaps dying because of faith in Me].

We all have a cross to bear; we must be willing to deny ourselves. We will not follow and run after Christ if we are not willing to deny ourselves. I remember a song years ago the older generation use to sing in church. "Must Jesus bear the cross alone and all the world go free? No there's a cross for everyone and there's a cross for me." Trust me, this is not always comfortable and it will take endurance to daily bear the cross and to continue to run looking unto Jesus. We must look unto Jesus for strength, courage, help and know he is our refuge. This is a day of reality for God's people to awaken and arise as the battle has only begun. We have tough days and challenges ahead and our love for God will be tried by fire. The word says after we are tried, we will come forth as pure gold. Job 23:10

These challenges are meant to purify us as we become the glorious church.

Let us remember the garden of Gethsemane in Matthew 26:36-39.

36 Then Jesus went with the disciples to a place called Gethsemane. He said to them, "Stay here while I go over there and pray."

37 He took Peter and Zebedee's two sons with him. He was beginning to feel deep anguish.38 Then he said to them, "My anguish is so great that I feel as if I'm dying. Wait here, and stay awake with me."

39 After walking a little farther, he quickly bowed with his face to the ground and prayed, "Father, if it's possible, let this cup of suffering be taken away from me. But your will be done rather than mine."

Gethsemane was a garden. I think of Gethsemane as a place of Jesus fiery trial, a place of suffering, and agony, a place where he denies himself and his interest. The meaning of Gethsemane is oil press. I remember hearing people say "I am pressed in Spirit." I have experienced that and understand I am in a divine confrontation with the Spirit of God and his dealings with me. I am being confronted with, "Is it going to be your will, Rochelle, or my will?" And that is the crossroad of the cross. Am I willing to lay my will down at the cross and submit myself unto his will? Trust me, we all will have those moments and even more so in these days and times. God is calling a bride, a people unto himself and that my friend, has cost. As Christ prayed in the garden, everything thing was pressed in him unto the will of his father. The scripture said he sweat blood. Oh my God! Those sweat drops of blood were for me and for you. We can see in the passage his interest while he was in the flesh. *"If it is possible let this cup pass, but not my will but yours be done."* Christ is our example. We all will have a Gethsemane moment that will prove us and demonstrate who we really love. My will or God's will – that is the question. These are serious moments of consideration as we look unto Jesus. Make no mistake, we will be tried.

As we look unto Jesus let us be encouraged by our patriarchs who obtained a good report by faith as they all came through trying times and moments such as Gethsemane. Let's take a look at these champions in Hebrews 11:32-40.

³²And what shall I more say? for the time would fail me to tell of Gedeon, and of Barak, and of Samson, and of Jephthae; of David also, and Samuel, and of the prophets:

³³Who through faith subdued kingdoms, wrought righteousness, obtained promises, stopped the mouths of lions.

³⁴Quenched the violence of fire, escaped the edge of the sword, out of weakness were made strong, waxed valiant in fight, turned to fight the armies of the aliens.

³⁵Women received their dead raised to life again: and others were tortured, not accepting deliverance; that they might obtain a better resurrection:

³⁶And others had trial of cruel mocking's and scourging's, yea, moreover of bonds and imprisonment:

³⁷They were stoned, they were sawn asunder, were tempted, were slain with the sword: they wandered about in sheepskins and goatskins; being destitute, afflicted, tormented;

³⁸(Of whom the world was not worthy:) they wandered in deserts, and in mountains, and in dens and caves of the earth.

³⁹And these all, having obtained a good report through faith, received not the promise:

[40]*God having provided some better thing for us, that they without us should not be made perfect.*

I can only shout when I read of these great Patriarchs of faith! They were lovers of God, looking unto Jesus. Now I'm sure I am going to step on some toes and silence some of this sugar gospel being preached. There are some who believe and even preach that once you say a prayer and accept Christ, that's all you have to do. You are bound for heaven. No, the word is clear when it says in Philippians 2:12 *"Wherefore, my beloved, as ye have always obeyed, not as in my presence only, but now much more in my absence, work out your own salvation with fear and trembling."* The best life now garbage that does not prepare you to become a warrior for the days ahead. Just like the patriarchs mentioned in Hebrews had to fight, it's no different for us. I grew up hearing "Don't worry, God's got it. Come by here Lord. He won't leave you. Jesus suffered with anguish and pain and died for us. You don't have to suffer if you have faith." I get it; all of that is true, but there is process. Our lives and journey will take us through process. In other words, the process will bring us to maturity in Christ and allow the living Christ to arise and be who he is in us. Now, getting back to the scripture - LOOK! Out of weaknesses they were made strong, escaped the edge of the sword, went through mocking and scourging, they were stoned, they were sawn asunder, were tempted, and were slain with the sword. Need I say more? Church, it's a part of the journey. *"And these all, having obtained a good report through faith, received not the promise: God having provided some better thing for us, that they without us should not be made perfect."* It says in verse 18 *"Of whom the world was not worthy."* What a testimony to have!

When I read about the heroes I am immediately brought back to Joan of Arc. I love Joan, her story and testimony. I remember my first English class in college I wrote about her and learned so much during my research. Before then, I really never knew much about her. Oh my, what a woman of God! She was a woman who gave her all to Christ. She stood against evil, slander, and lies. She died at the stake because she was considered a heretic. She did not escape the edge of the sword but received a good report. She knew her God and never denied him. Rather she looked unto Jesus. See, my friends, these things are real, War is real. I'm talking about the unseen war that Ephesians 6:12 speaks of.

For we wrestle not against flesh and blood, but against principalities, against powers, against the rulers of the darkness of this world, against spiritual wickedness in high places.

Are we aware we are in a war? It's unseen. It's not with people, rulers or governments but against powers of darkness. Even if we are not aware, Satan and his demons are aware and they will take advantage of our ignorance. Always remember - the devil thrives on ignorance. It's one of his greatest tools. It's time the church awakens and gets dressed for war and become the warrior bride Christ intends it to become.

It will be no different for us in these end days. It may not be as severe as those mentioned above but we all have a cross and will be faced with many battles, burdens, stress and trouble. As I said before, it's a part of the journey. Oh, but the Christ within is the over-comer in us if we allow him to be. These are days we must awake. Days of ease are over. Some may read this and think 'God is mean. Why would he allow this?' As I said, our lives must go though process to reach his will for our lives. Like the scripture said above they not being perfect apart from us because GOD HAS SOMETHING BETTER! I began to learn and experience some of this in my earlier days. I would pray and ask God to remove this or that from my life, because it was causing so much pain. I heard the Lord say so plain "I am not doing nothing you ask me because I am killing you." Talk about shock and awe in my life! He was breaking my strong will, my will to govern my own life even after I had said "Yes Lord." Now that I look back, I see that he had something better for my life that I would not have received had he honored my request. Christ allowed me to go through the process. What is the meaning of the word process? It is a series of actions that you take in order to achieve a result. Actions, I might add, that are not comfortable. No! I don't like the process but it's God's way or no way. I must say I love the results that come as I go through the process.

I am certain some may only be hearing this for the first time and it may be hard to understand and comprehend. But if you are serious about God, he will teach and train. I would say he will do a quick work in you if you are willing to fully and completely lay down your own life. There's really no other way. My prayer is that in some way things I have penned in this book will help someone. The hour is late, church. We have reached a point where the Lord is saying, "It's time to choose sides. If you are for me, come to this side. Those who are not for me, go to the other side." He's calling his bride out to make her ready. Will you be a candidate? Will you totally surrender all you are to Christ? If so, he awaits you. There is no other way, my friend. Look unto Jesus the author and finisher of our faith. Lift up your head for your redemption draws nigh. MARANATHA!

The Coin of Life

I n walking with the Lord, I have come to understand that when he gives me specific topics to journal or write it is not for me to gain mere information but to put into practice what I am learning as he is teaching me. Christ must be experienced in all of our lives and he is experienced when we take his word, the living word that he is and put into practice daily in a practical way.

My mandate from the Lord when directing me to pen books is in journal form and simplicity to make it easy for people to comprehend which leads to walking it out through daily living. I find that the Lord is and has been very specific with the different topic to write and ones that are most needed for the times we are living in. Some information may be new to some but old to others but we must be careful to not let earthy wisdom steer us away from the word of the Lord because we do not agree, believe or understand it. God's word will always be truth. I encourage the reader to take the scriptures used in these journals and study them out further. We can never exhaust the word of God unto total and complete understanding because God is eternal. We will forever be learning until we leave the earth and then beyond.

Life in some ways can be compared to spending a coin, or at least in my depiction. Each day we rise, we have a coin, the gift of life to spend however we choose. Our life is ours, it is up to us to spend it anyway we want. The coin I am referring to is the coin of free will. God has given us a free will that he will not violate. Likewise we should not allow anyone or entity to violate our free will.

I am sure someone may ask, how is this coin spent? A person spends a coin daily by his decisions and choices, how he lives, the words he speaks, deeds sown. It is just like the talent in the Bible. The Lord gave each servant a talent, a coin. Though some servants had more than others, each was responsible to increase on what was given, or better said to make good on a return. After a period, the owner came back to see what his servant had done with what he had given and judged accordingly.

At the end of each day, we have spent our coin. Hopefully our deeds, words, and actions increased and produced a harvest of Christ. Our goal is to make a good return for the Lord. The fruits produced and released should honor HIM not US. Hopefully, not our wrong decisions, choices and words, have not brought dishonor to his name.. Of course, not all days are perfect or as we would desire because we contend with our flesh, but thank God for his blood and the forgiveness of sins that we may commit. God so loves us and his love covers a multitude of sin. Yes! And amen.

The point is: life is short, and none of us know when we will take our last breath and leave this earth. The way we have spent our coin matters. In the end we will receive our final reward and return to the throne of God on judgment day. We cannot afford to put off today thinking we can do it tomorrow for truly, none of us know if there is tomorrow. Tomorrow could very well be today. Let us awaken from our slumber. Romans 13:11 NLT nailed it. *"This is more urgent, for you know how late it is; time is running out. Wake up, for our salvation is nearer now than when we first believed."*

In closing, I would like to ask a question. If you died right at this moment, do you know where you would end up? Would your daily coin of life have been spent for you to obtain the big heavenly jackpot? Will you earn the reward of eternity with Christ? Will you hear the words *"Well done thy good and faithful servant you have been faithful over a few things come on up a little higher and I will make you ruler of many?"* Let none of us answer too quickly but allow time for reflection of our lives and allow the purifier Christ to come in and purify our hearts and mind that we will not be bankrupt at his appearing.

Now that we have taken care of the money issue and how to spend it, let's begin our journey unto an awakening together.

A Note from the Author

Dear reader, Brothers and Sisters in Christ. It has been my pleasure and great honor that you would take the time to read my book and go on this journey with me. I pray that Christ was able to come through me his vessel, his daughter of Zion and help light your path along the way. I may not personally know you but I love and appreciate you.

I encourage you in the days ahead to take courage in Christ alone and become madly in love with him that no price or anything he would ask of you would be too great. Wherever you are in your walk with the Lord keep moving and stay consistent. Do not become weary in well doing for you will reap if you faint not. Don't let the small foxes such as frustration distract you because results you are looking for may not appear when you want, but just know God does hear and answer prayer. Things are swiftly changing and we all must hold to God's unchanging hand in the days ahead and stay in the fight. I will be in the fight with you. As the people of God held up Moses' hand to win the battle let us hold each other in prayer and realize we are the bride Christ will return for. May we keep our lamps trimmed and burning bright.

I pray you heard and can hear the sounding of the trumpet! Having done all to stand STAND on the foundation of Christ. Be Blessed now and always! Maranatha!

GG-God's Girl!

www.ingramcontent.com/pod-product-compliance
Lightning Source LLC
Chambersburg PA
CBHW020452130626
46549CB00001B/389